SUMMER 1999
EDIT
PRODUCTION STEPHEN TROUSSÉ
ADVERTISING LISA ROBERTS

CONTENTS

Further Adventures in the 20th Century
pages 3 – 79

Editorial; Andrew Motion interviewed by Jane Hardy (4); poem by Andrew Motion (8); The Sonnet History: John Whitworth on The Laureateship (11); Roberto Galaverni on the legacy of futurism (12); poems by Maurizio Cucchi (16), Claudio Damiani (17), Andrea Gibellini (19), Davide Rondoni (20), Valerio Magrelli (23); Peter Forbes on Montale (24); Carol Rumens on the conversation of Joseph Brodsky (25); two poems by Alla Gelich (27); poem by Eugene Dubnov (29); Andrew Zawacki on Tomaz Salamun (30); poem by Tomaz Salamun (35).

Poems
36 – 51

by Tom Paulin, Mark Halliday (38), M. R. Peacocke (39), Charles Boyle (40), Billy Collins (41), Helen Dunmore (43), Frances Sackett (44), Adam Thorpe (45), Linda Saunders (46), Keith Jebb (47), Justo Jorge Padrón (48), Sheenagh Pugh (49), George Szirtes (50), Vernon Scannell (51)

A Second Look
52 – 57

Peter Bland on Brian Jones; Stephen Burt on Randall Jarrell (54); poem by Stephen Burt

German Poetry
58 – 60

Lawrence Sail on Günter Grass; poems by Georg Trakl (59) and Robert Saxton (60)

Polish Poetry
61 – 62

poems by Zbigniew Herbert and Piotr Sommer (62)

Robert Frost
63 – 64

Jay Parini's biography reviewed by Vernon Scannell

The Classic Poem
65 – 66

James Keery on Burns Singer

Appreciation
66 – 67

Gael Turnbull on William Price Turner

The Review Pages
68 – 88

Stephen Romer on Geoffrey Hill; David Wheatley on Philip Gross, Jo Shapcott, Fred D'Aguiar, Robert Crawford, Stephen Romer (71); Kate Clanchy on Rita Dove (75); Ian McMillan on The Bloodaxe Quartets audio-books (77); Sheenagh Pugh on Louise Glück (78); Helen Dunmore on Carol Ann Duffy (80); Edwin Morgan on Richard Price (82); Dennis O' Driscoll on Tomas Tranströmer (83); Ruth Padel on Linda Pastan (84); Adam Thorpe on D. J. Enright (85); Atar Hadari on Michael Ondaatje (86); Michael Hulse on Michael Hofmann (87)

Poems
89 – 94

by Charles Tomlinson, Andrew Waterman (90), Elizabeth Bartlett, (91), Michael Henry (92), Hugh Macpherson (93), Pete Morgan (94)

Endstops
95 – 96

News and Comment, Net Verse, Letters

All illustrations by Gerald Mangan

Feminist Review

THE UK'S LEADING FEMINIST JOURNAL

Special Poetry Issue
Issue 62, June 1999
Edited by Vicki Bertram

Contemporary Women Poets

'Older Sisters are very Sobering Things': contemporary women poets and the female affiliation complex - *Jane Dowson*

The Woman Poet's Dilemma: Eavan Boland's classic essay reconsidered twelve years on - *Sarah Maguire*

The Therapeutic Uses of Poetry - *Gillie Bolton*

Contemporary British Lesbian Poetry: an exploration - *Liz Yorke*

Why Experimental Poetry is Good for Women - *Harriet Tarlo*

Round Table Discussion on Poetry in Performance - *Jean Binta Breeze, Patience Agbabi, Jillien Tipene, Ruth Harrison & Vicki Bertram*

For further information or to order this Special Issue of *Feminist Review*, **Contemporary Women Poets**, please contact Justine Sansom at:

Tel: +44 (0)1235 401000
Fax: +44 (0)1235 401550
E-mail: justines@carfax.co.uk

Routledge/Taylor & Francis Ltd
PO Box 25 • Abingdon • Oxfordshire
OX14 3UE • UK
Visit the Taylor & Francis Home Page at
http://www.tandf.co.uk

EDITORIAL AND BUSINESS ADDRESS:
22 BETTERTON STREET, LONDON WC2H 9BU

telephone   0171 420 9880
fax   0171 240 4818
email   poetrysoc@dial.pipex.com
website   http://www.poetrysoc.com

POETRY REVIEW
SUBSCRIPTIONS
Four issues including postage:

UK individuals £27
Overseas individuals £35
(all overseas delivery is by airmail)
USA individuals $56

Libraries, schools and institutions:
UK £35
Overseas £42
USA $66

Single issue £6.95 + 50p p&p (UK)

Sterling and US dollar payments only. Eurocheques, Visa and Mastercard payments are acceptable.

Bookshop distribution:
Signature
Telephone 0161 834 8767

Design by Philip Lewis
Cover image: 'Elasticity' 1916 (oil on canvas) by Umberto Boccioni (1882–1916) Pinacoteca di Brera, Milan, Italy/Bridgeman Art Library

Typeset by Poetry Review.

Printed by Grillford Ltd at
26 Peverel Drive, Bletchley,
Milton Keynes MK1 1QZ
Telephone: 01908 644123

POETRY REVIEW is the magazine of the Poetry Society. It is published quarterly and issued free to members of the Poetry Society. Poetry Review considers submissions from non-members and members alike. To ensure reply submissions must be accompanied by an SAE or adequate International Reply coupons: Poetry Review accepts no responsibility for contributions that are not reply paid.

Founded 24 February 1909
Charity Commissioners No: 303334
© 1999

FURTHER ADVENTURES IN THE 20TH CENTURY

BY PETER FORBES

"HISTORY HAS MANY cunning passages…" said Eliot. And so has poetic history. Most poetry magazines most of the time stick to the straight and narrow of the mainstream: the received canonical poets of the recent past and the names currently making waves. But with the millennium looming it seemed a good idea to look at some neglected corners.

Italian poetry has not been widely read in Britain in recent years and traffic between the two poetries has not been high, bar a few shining exceptions, such as Montale. But things are changing. The New Generation Poets promotion was noticed in Italy and poets like Simon Armitage and Carol Ann Duffy are being translated. The poems we have had translated for this issue come from Italy's equivalent to *The New Poetry*, Roberto Galaverni's *Nuovi Poeti Italiani Contemporanei*, and collections by Maurizio Cucchi and Davide Rondoni, which were brought to our notice by Luca Guerneri, Seamus Heaney's Italian translator. He has acted as general adviser on the Italian section. Roberto Galaverni himself has contributed an article on futurism, as a contribution to the current re-assessment of Modernism taking place in various quarters.

It is strange to reflect that at a time when poets hardly notice the pace of modern life, beyond slipping occasional references to jet lag into poems, or musing on a train, that in the early century, when no vehicle travelled much faster that 20 miles an hour, the futurists whipped themselves up into ecstasies about speed and power and the coming of the new metallized man. As Roberto Galaverni points out, futurism discredited itself politically rather than aesthetically by finding in fascism a political programme that seem to suit its own aims.

But there are still lessons in futurism: the aim was to write poetry that reflected the life of the cities (and perhaps it found its apotheosis not in Italian poetry at all but in Pessoa), and it is paradoxical that in this country, as the futurist century ends, the two most admired poets – Heaney and Hughes – are poets of the countryside rather than the city.

It is true that Hughes applied imagery from science and technology to nature but the focus of his attention was not the city. It is hard to believe that the 21st century will continue this anti-urban bias.

Brian Jones is exactly the kind of good poet who tends to get forgotten in the current climate. Even his publisher Michael Schmidt, has omitted him from his *Harvill Book of Twentieth-Century Poetry in English*. But Jones is an excellent chronicler of the less glamorous side of the '60s and '70s, and his best poems deserve a place in the anthologies. Randall Jarrell has never been forgotten but a case still needs to be made for his poetry.

Bill Turner, who died last year, was an underrated poet par excellence. He had two careers in a sense because he changed his name from William Price Turner to Bill Turner in 1979. Under neither name did he achieve true recognition but he was one of stalwarts of the little magazine world, a fine, independent and irascible reviewer (often in these pages) and a poet with a distinctive playful/lugubrious voice that still deserves to find readers. Gael Turnbull's appreciation is on page 66.

There isn't much left to say about Andrew Motion's appointment as Poet Laureate except to note how widely the "bag of shite" attack was noticed/deprecated. As Philip Hensher said in the *Spectator*, "a stone was lifted, and underneath, unsuspected, was a swarming mass of life…". The episode was a warning that there is something rotten in the state of Poesia and that a siege mentality can breed some very ugly moods in those trapped behind their self-erected barricades.

The Hands-On Laureate

JANE HARDY INTERVIEWS ANDREW MOTION

SINCE ANDREW MOTION became Poet Laureate in May, bookshops have sold out of his work. Faber are busy reprinting his poetry and biographies (of Keats, Philip Larkin, Edward Thomas) and this interview was slotted in after lunch with Culture Secretary Chris Smith. The shrill sound of faxes arriving punctuated our chat. That's what it means to be Poet Laureate at the tail end of the twentieth century. Motion lives in a large house in Tufnell Park with his second wife Jan Dalley and their children. We talked in his eyrie of a study where he writes poems down longhand in black ink before transcribing them onto a word processor.

JH: Did you want to be Poet Laureate, or a poet of renown, very early on?

AM: I didn't want to be Poet Laureate as a little boy! I really didn't think of it in those terms. And to say I wanted to become a poet "of renown" aged 14 would make me seem even more odious than I probably was at that age. But as soon as I started writing poems in earnest, which was slightly later, in my first A level year, I almost immediately felt my life was possessed by poetry. It was in the early days of Careers Advice in schools and I remember this person saying to me, "What are you going to do when you grow up?" and me saying, "I am a poet" in a preposterous way. He said, "Well, there's nothing to say to you then". I'm telling this story against myself, but it goes to show I did feel very devoted to it.

JH: Why do you think you felt this strong a commitment?

AM: Partly because nobody else in the school (Radley College, near Oxford) was interested in poetry, and partly because nobody read much in my family. So there was no expectation of my being interested in that kind of thing. It never crossed my mind that my devotion to poetry would somehow translate into a public version of itself. And yet even then, the question of who might read the stuff occurred to me. Do you write for yourself? Are you writing for your friends? Are you writing to try to get your girlfriend to give you a kiss? The question of the audience and the society for poems was there in a very inchoate form.

JH: What was your first achieved poem?

AM: I wrote almost every day at school – poems of absolutely no distinction whatever. Can I remember any lines? Well, they didn't really have lines, they just went on about me-me-me. My life, my anxieties, absolutely typical adolescent inverted peerings and probings. I was reading French Symbolist poets mainly, which didn't do much for my logic, but a lot for my addiction to words. I was just spilling over with words. Then my mother had her terrible accident, and it just unavoidably presented me with a subject. It sounds cold-hearted to say it, but it focussed these adolescent ramblings...

But to answer your question at last: the first

poem I pushed out and thought, That's better, is a little poem called 'In the Attic' which I wrote when I was 20. It took about thirty seconds to write. I'd been reading *The Hawk in the Rain* and my new first wife and I were living in the country outside Oxford in the attic of an old rectory, living on love and cider.

JH: Were you pleased?

AM: I felt an accelerated version of what I always feel when I want to write: I mean, that feeling Frost describes so beautifully as "a lump in the throat, a lovesickness, a homesickness". It's the feeling that there's something which has already existed, that you're trying to remember. And when I wrote 'In the Attic' I thought: It's better organised, it more nearly captured that past sense. I also thought: If I've done it once, maybe I can do it again. But that's one of the delusions of youth – that if you can do it once, you're already on a steady upward trajectory. It ain't like that.

JH: You refer to this experience, you mother's riding accident and death, in many of your poems dealing with other kinds of love, your wife, your children. Do you think there's a kind of survivor's guilt?

AM: I honestly think that if she'd been killed instantly, we might not be having this conversation. What was especially grim was that she was betwixt and between for ten years, not really alive and not quite dead. So we couldn't post the parcel of our grief. What I've tried to do, in poetic terms and as a way of getting through my life, is concentrate very precisely on the facts of the accident, make them as telling and revelatory as possible, but also to use what happened as a way of characterising a whole range of experience that might not refer to her at all. In other words, to try and understand or re-describe it as a view of the world – a view which encompasses randomness, the point of suffering, generational issues and with the sense of all our lives heading in one direction: towards death. These are the subjects of poets though the ages, but I think my intense longing to go on writing about those things has as much to do with the fact that she went on suffering for such a long time, as it has to do with the accident itself.

JH: In your earliest book, *Goodnestone* (Workshop New Poetry, 1972) you write "The weight of love / Is what loads me down". Do you agree there's often a quotient of pain in your view of love?

AM: I'm afraid that's probably true. The poem I wrote for my wife, Jan, 'On the Table' is a bit more cheerful. But my view of poetry generally attracts me to subjects which have a sense of loss or deprivation or unfulfillment. Over the years, I have tried to enlarge the reference, so that it's not just a case of my sitting down and saying me-me-me as I did when I was young. I feel what Keats talks about when he says, "Axioms of Philosophy not being Axioms until they're proved upon our pulses" is completely right. I want to take the particular examples of grief, suffering, loss that I have encountered, and more recently the experience of being ill myself, and present them as a larger picture of what I think life is like. And I'm afraid I do think life is like that. It doesn't mean I am incapable of being happy, though I think as you get older, it gets more difficult. I think your capacity for joy, for *jouissance*, is diminished. It's a long time since I had any of those careless laughing raptures. (He laughed).

JH: Seamus Heaney talked about the Laureate creating a "sacred space" for poetry, Larkin refused what he dubbed the "representing-British-poetry in the 'Poetry Conference at Belgrade' side of it". What's your job description?

AM: I think that Heaney, like Hughes, has a very well developed sense of what Ted called "the sacred trust of poetry" – and although it's a grand phrase, I want to say "So do I". Whatever our feelings about monarchy, whatever your politics, whatever your poetic politics, we ought to be able to agree that poetry does have an element of sacred trust about it. One of the things I want to do is defend poetry in the most general way. I think part of the pleasure of the job of Laureate is that there isn't a job description. Effectively, it comes in two parts – there's the doing part and the writing part. The writing part has a better developed tradition around it; you write poems for royal occasions sometimes, depending on whether you can. I'm very keen to make those poems part of a larger pattern of poems about public events. Events in the life of the nation, political things. On the other hand, there's the doing bit, which has less of a tradition. Some Poet Laureates have done a lot, some have done absolutely nothing. I intend to do a very great deal – I'm going to get closely involved in educational matters, raising the profile of poetry in schools. I've got all kinds of meetings lined up with everybody from The Poetry Society through to the Department of Education and the British Council. I've also got ideas for independent initiatives, to do with raising money to provide places where poets can go to do their work uninterrupted. I want to edit a regular series of poems about national events, solicited from well-known poets and people who haven't published before. I want to do a gigantic anthology for schools called *The Poetry Book*. I want to persuade Radio 3 or 4 or both to have a regular series of poetry lectures with programmes introducing the work of other writers. I also want to wake up the committee of the Queen's Gold Medal for Poetry and possibly make that a big annual event.

JH: John Betjeman wrote a good poem on 'The Death of George V' before becoming Laureate, a terrible 'Ballad on the Investiture 1969' after his appointment. Are you worried about the effect on the quality of your work?

AM: It doesn't quite worry me, but it certainly concerns me. I am aware it's a completely no-win situation: I'm damned if I do, damned if I don't. I've thought about that and about the flak-taking. And I thought a lot about the invasion of my private space. I decided there was something so interesting and creative to do for the whole community of poets, I'd take the risk. I think the stimulation to write other kinds of poetry might actually be rather good for me.

JH: You have said you want to broaden the role of Laureate to be a kind of voice for the nation, speaking on national questions. Have you written anything about the Kosovan war?

AM: I've been commissioned recently by the Endellion quartet to write poems to go between the sections of Haydn's *Seven Last Words*, which will be performed next year. It's a very exciting, beguiling task – seven sections, about 1,000 lines in all. One of the sections is about the Kosovan refugees. How extractable it is, I don't know. It's the life story of a pushchair which is wheeled out of some ethnically cleansed village, then is dumped in a refugee camp. It's not about the people, although they are all around, it's just about the pushchair. We'll see how it works. I must say, I do want to engage with great public issues, but I believe Keats was right again when he said: we hate poetry which has a palpable design on us. It's almost invariably true that poems which deal best with public events are poems which don't come at them like a bull at a gate. The best poems about the troubles in Northern Ireland, for instance, are not poems about bombs going off in pubs, but Seamus Heaney's poems about bog people. You have to find a way for proceeding in your intended direction by indirections. For a poet like me, who is quiet and personal and yes, private, it is quite a test to write about public things. I have to find a private way to tackle them. If I were more of a rhymster, a Tony Harrison, I'd find a way to aim at them more directly. But I'm not, can't be and I don't want to be.

JH: 'Lines of Desire' is about your affection for Wilfred Owen and Edward Thomas and your feelings about war. Anthony Thwaite describes your poetry as "traditionalist", yet you're experimental here. Is that the wrong adjective for your poetry?

AM: It is odd that I'm always described as traditional when in fact I'm not. To be honest, I look at the poems in *Selected Poems* – 'Lines of Desire' and 'Salt Water' and several others – and I think: well, these aren't traditional exactly, though they might be interested in tradition. One of the odd things about the past few days is that I now feel there's another Andrew Motion going around in the newspapers who is barely recognisable. And I don't just mean, although this is part of the problem, that his age is wrong, the names of his friends and his family are wrong, the dates are wrong – the account of the poems is wrong!

JH: The response to your appointment has been predictably mixed: some enthusiastic, some critical. On the negative side, the Andrew Motion that's emerged could be described as a possibly-bisexual-Establishment-not-good-enough-poet-biographer, couldn't he?

AM: My sense of it all is this: there was a lot of begrudging during the first week, when I was fortunately out of the country. Then it steeply turned round, with much more friendly things being written.

JH: Do you want to correct the political inaccuracy. Would you have accepted the job of Laureate under a Conservative Government?

AM: I think so, if I could have controlled the job description. But it's questionable whether I would have been offered it, since I've been a member of the Labour Party for a long time.

JH: Have you started writing the *epithalamium* (wedding poem) for Prince Edward yet? Do you think a traditional form such as a sonnet will suit this commission?

AM: I can't really say without having written the poem. But I'm inclined to think a traditional form would work. When I was asked to write the Diana poem – which is something else everybody gets wrong – it wasn't a convulsion by me, but a commission I was happy to accept, I immediately found myself thinking the way to do it best was to drop into some lapidary, Housmanish, blocked-off, stanzaic form. Partly because writing in strict form helps you to a thought, as somebody said, but also because it has a kind of dignity which helps. I can see myself using quite conventional forms for these sorts of poems.

JH: Wouldn't it also help you avoid poems like Ted Hughes' work about the Queen Mother?

AM; The furious, devout, drench poem, you mean? Well, although Ted got a lot of flak for his Laureate poems, I think he was onto something very interesting, trying to look beyond the personalities involved to something – in his sense of the word – primitive. A connection between poetry and monarchy, between monarchy and landscape. A Pike-like Englishness which was always his subject.

JH: You are also in charge of the University of East Anglia's famous creative writing course. Do you think poetry is an art or a craft, and can writing be taught?

AM: I don't think it's possible to make something from nothing, but since the people on my course are already so good by the time they join, this isn't a problem. The standard of applicants is really very high, with about 500 applying for about 40 places. Some of them don't need much help at all, but even these need editing. With those who are in more of a muddle, I can do more substantial work, saying: You need a new character here, or Your descriptive writing is no good. I'm in Norwich two days a week and I love it. It's important for me to have a base outside London. I love the landscape – surprising for a supposedly metropolitan poet!

JH: A kind of poetry war was posited by the media, with opposite forces headed by you and Carol Ann Duffy. Did it bother you?

AM: I have the greatest respect for Carol Ann Duffy as a person and as a poet. To suggest there's bad blood between her and me is ridiculous. I regret it's been presented like this. It's Press mischief. I've spent a lot of time over the last years tearing down the barriers which did exist between schools of poets, and hope in future to make sure they stay down. This imagined opposition between types of poet is largely garbage, as is the phrase "people's poet". Is Benjamin Zephaniah more or less of a people's poet than Seamus Heaney? It's a false dichotomy. We live in a poetic society that is happily as diverse as our political society.

JH: How does a poem begin for you? Obviously the poems for Haydn's *Seven Last Words* were a commission, but how did you start?

AM: Poems really do begin with that inarticulate longing to rehabilitate something that's been forgotten or vanquished. It's a music I start with, sad music, without words. Then an idea I've got in my conscious mind attaches itself – or something I've read or heard. Before I start writing in my notebook, I've written about half the poem in my head, often in the middle of the night, when the children were small. I still sleep badly and often write in the night. It's reassuring to have the first half of a poem in my head before I sort it out on the page. It means I'm paying attention to the sound and gives confidence, like the run-up to a jump. I revise a lot on the page and a lot after a poem has appeared in a magazine, before it's in a book. I even rewrote quite a lot of the poems in *Selected Poems*.

JH: Did you become sparer?

AM: Clearer. What irritated me about my earlier poems was that they kept going out of focus. Going off at a bit of a tangent now: one of the things I've always felt is that writing is bliss compared to speaking. You have the chance of

> It is odd that I'm always described as traditional when in fact I'm not. To be honest, I look at the poems in *Selected Poems* – 'Lines of Desire' and 'Salt Water' and several others – and I think: well, these aren't traditional exactly, though they might be interested in tradition.

getting right what you want to say. When you're speaking in interviews and elsewhere, there are so many other pressures which don't exist when you're writing. I feel a completely free agent – it's quiet, it's free, I'm completely my own person. If some people don't like what I write, I feel that I won't be surprised; there'll be others who will. Which in turn prompts me to say: I'm always being described as a quiet-voiced, mild-mannered sort of person. But in fact most things I've done in my life have caused a row of one sort or another. There was a row about the Penguin anthology, a row about the Larkin book, a row about the Keats book – with people who don't like politics with their poetry. I have always believed valuable things happen at the point of an argument. Be your own person and time will sort the rest out.

JH: Are you a poet or biographer?

AM: I'm a poet who writes biography. I am interested in biography, probably because I'm a person who has an adequate imagination but not much power of invention. With biography, you're given the plot. But poetry is central to my existence and dictates the shape of every day. The other work I do is taken because it's flexible enough to allow me to write poetry.

JH: Keats, Edward Thomas and Philip Larkin are the subjects of your three greatest biographies. Is there a link?

AM: Maybe. Although I'm very admiring of Keats' poetry, it's his Letters I feel closest to. I revered Edward Thomas and his long sinuous sentences, which play the unit of the sentence against the unit of a phrase and the unit of the rhyme. I've learnt a lot from Thomas. Larkin is a more robust, more direct poet. I'm sure I have taken things from him too, but I'm not sure what. It's good for poets not to be too canny about their thefts and borrowings; such things relate to the side of the mind that needs to remain unconscious – the primeval swamp side.

JH: What is your ambition now?

AM: I've no higher ambition than to write a poem that someone wants to read in 100 years.

JH: Which of your poems is that likely to be?

AM: The one I'm going to write next! It's hard to tell, poems have odd lives. The ones that do most in the short term don't necessarily last. Although some, like 'Dover Beach' or 'In Memoriam' arrive impressively and endure for ever.

JH: Will you be able to retain the subversive nature of a poet's activity?

AM: I think poetry means writing against the grain, writing in borrowed time. There's an unsubmissiveness about it. Although I'll be using my time as Poet Laureate to make things happen, I want to make sure I "speak truth to power" as Hazlitt said. Poetry should never speak on behalf of power.

ANDREW MOTION
TERRITORIAL

The war ended. My father's war went on
In a Territorial twilight: one-off dances
(which meant scarlet jackets and drainpipes)
and dull drill at week-ends: close by in Colchester,

or further off and more exciting on Dartmoor.
"The Yeo-boys" was my mother's word for them,
"Yeo-boys; soldier boys; his boys", half-resentful
and half in awe, which in turn meant whenever

I heard the gravel-squirt of his car swirling
home into the yard, I felt the same, caught
somewhere between a thrill and a warning.
Live up to him. Think what he went through.

Then the car went quiet and there he was
in our dim doorway, waiting for me to go to him,
my father, his uniform smart as a shop manikin's,
his Sam Browne slashing his chest like a sword-cut.

What had I been doing, he wanted to know,
which I see now was fair enough. In those days
I supposed it meant: do you deserve the life
you've got – which made me stare beyond him

at the post-and-rails glimmering outside,
at the level hay field, at the scrawny line
of elders and other weed-trees by the road,
and feel my head empty. When I came to,

we were still in the dark hall, with him
hanging on my shoulder but now scanning ahead
for my mother, cooking supper in her kitchen
with the light off, appreciating the money saved.

Another time, we would be away to Dartmoor,
my mother and I standing under a tall hedge
and protected by that - out of the wind –
as well as the posse of sharp uniforms

which haw-hawed and jaw-jawed with her,
and now and again tousled my hair heavily,
 telling me one day I too might "like to have a go
in that" - "that" being the Armed Personnel Carrier

which had my invisible father bouncing inside it
as it nipped about on the olive green below us,
giving bucks and stumbles when it hit tussocks,
and occasionally firing off rounds of blanks.

I could tell this, because the perky gun barrel
sometimes coughed a cigarette-smoke breath –
though the bang only reached me seconds later,
and anyway the thing was too like a toy

to be true, or like a film, or a run-together series
of frames in a war comic – the kind I often read,
where I knew how the war ended, but never saw
the end itself, only the same faces fighting on and on

over the same black ground, where days rushed
forward in jagged frames, but somehow stood still.
It felt like my duty, but how could I hope
to join their story? That was just one question

I could not settle, and there were others as well:
Was I brave? Would the son be less than the father?
What was the father's gift to the son? Recently,
as it happened, a small silver-plated pen-knife

which I loved – practising miniature bayonettings
and stabbings in our hay-shed, where the bales
were stacked floor to ceiling each late summer,
the top ones whiskered by spiders in the rafters,

the bottom ones squashed. They wore down like soft rocks
as we carted them off one by one to the stables
after mucking-out, and I sliced on with my virgin blade
until in due course the knife slipped from my hand

into a scratchy bay-ravine, its silver winking back
while it vanished, reminding me even then of a horse
my father had told me about, a cavalry horse
with one of his Yeo-boys up top, pulling a gun-carriage

and galloping at full tilt across a flat patch of Dartmoor,
at full tilt and in full view of him and others,
which one minute was brilliant and flying in glory –
the glossy chestnut mare, the gleaming green gun-barrel,

the spattered but polished carriage, and the fellow astride
swaying masterfully, reins taut but not too much so –
and the next was slithering into a marsh which had lain
hidden under its furry moss lid for centuries,

with skinny-legged birds landing safely,
nothing else, and which now swallowed horse,
gun, carriage and last of all man, his wild white eye
the final thing to go, but soon entirely gone.

ANDREW MOTION
THE SONNET HISTORY

JOHN WHITWORTH
ANDY-PANDY, PUDDING AND PIE

When the Nation's professoriate were searching for a laureate
(The grand chams and the little chams all cogitating hard),
Down the corridors of power, growing stronger by the hour,
Came the notion: ANDREW MOTION, he's the business, he's the bard.

Elegiac-epic-lyric, dithyrambical-satiric,
Macaronic-catatonic, he's your feller, he's your man,
As the critics cut up rougher and the going's getting tougher,
Andy's handy, send for Andy, he can do it, yes he can.

Andy's handy, send for Andy, he's the vintage, he's the brandy,
Other poets (don't you know it?) are the smallest of small beer,
Mad 'uns, sad 'uns, bad 'uns, funny 'uns, only Andy knows his onions,
Po-confession's his profession, he's the sage of souvenir.

At the Ministry of Leisure Andy *steams* to do your pleasure,
He's your Poet By Appointment – stanzas cut and made to measure.

Back to Futurismo

ROBERTO GALAVERNI RE-EXAMINES THE MOVEMENT
THAT INITIATED EUROPEAN LITERARY MODERNISM

WHEN WE SPEAK of futurism we must remember first of all of its initiator Filippo Tommaso Marinetti (1876-1944), to whose breakthrough we owe the birth and development of the first great movement of the European avant-garde. The importance of futurism lies in this European beginning and in its status as the first organized artistic and cultural movement, the founding father of the avant-garde idea which runs through the century in various artforms, not only in literature. It is significant that the first compositions in the new mode (poetic compositions in free verse, drama and fiction) were drafted in French and that the first Futurist Manifesto itself was published in *Le Figaro* of February 1909, before being published in Italian translation in *Poesia*, the Milan review which Marinetti himself had founded in 1905.

The original germ of futurism, therefore, should not be characterised simply as a brilliant and subversive intuition of a writer of exuberant creative energy, but should be understood in its systematic and programmatic aspect as a collective poetic capable of reaching not only beyond the national border of Italy but also into other artistic fields such as painting and music, thanks to the tenacity and initiative of a group of more or less faithful friends and disciples who developed Marinetti's original idea. From the beginning then, futurism presents itself as, not the singular and unrepeatable experience of artistic individuals but as an organic episode, albeit with individual quirks, and as an all-embracing avant-garde movement that very quickly spread from France and Italy throughout all of Europe. Above all it comprised a great rebellious or revolutionary leap, nonconformist vitality, the collective engagement of its supporters, and the subversive energy of its youthful impetus. It will suffice to refer to a passage in which the great father-figure Marinetti, in the same spirit and rhetoric that the movement extols, recalls his futurist colleagues, to realise how the generational and vitalistic spirit infuses the reflective pieces and the entire orbit of their artistic programme: "Hail! great incendiary poets, my futurist brothers... Hail! Paolo Buzzi, Gian Pietro Lucini, Palazzeschi, Govoni, Altomare, Folgore, Cardile, Boccioni, Carrà, Russolo, Balla, Severini, Pratella, D'Alba, Mazza, Carrieri, Frontini! We are leaving paralysis behind, we are ravaging Podagra, and rolling out the great military railroad on the flanks of Gorisankar, the summit of the world!" Moreover, futurism appears like the celebration of the so-called *Erlebnis*, as the exaltation of the new against all received tradition, of the ability to continually surpass each achievement, of the refusal of all stability and all hierarchy, of continuous invention.

The origins of the futurist movement then cannot be separated from a very distinctive historical context, with two dominant factors: development and the progress of science and in particular technology in the context of the delayed Italian industrial revolution (in such a sense the thematic and figurative innovation of futurism is that it replaces as a fit object of attention the agricultural landscape and typical peasant of the Italian tradition by the industrial and urban world), and the first dark skirmishes of the great world-wide conflict that was already on the horizon. The two elements reinforced each other because the celebration of

FROM THE FUTURIST MANIFESTO

1. We want to sing the love of danger, the habit of energy and rashness.

2. The essential elements of our poetry will be courage, audacity and revolt.

3. Literature has up to now magnified pensive immobility, ecstasy and slumber. We want to exalt movements of aggression, feverish sleeplessness, the double march, the perilous leap, the slap and the blow with the fist.

4. We declare that the splendour of the world has been enriched by a new beauty: the beauty of speed.

innovation, of speed, of impersonality associated with the creatures of the new technology, achieved a kind of terrible apotheosis in the idea of a technological war dominated by equipment that would test the "new man" in the starkest possible way on the fields of the western front (already in one of his best known poems Marinetti celebrates the battle of Adrianopolis, which took place in 1912 during the first Balkan war).

It is no accident that the growth of the ideas of the futurist movement should have happened almost exclusively in the great cities, Milan above all, but also in Florence, and that only in the cities did the futurists organize genuine cultural activity. In particular in Florence, the authentic literary capital, there began to grow up some groups around the review *Voce* which was characterized by a great ethical and civil commitment and open to other fields of interest beyond the literary. These then gave place in 1913 to the new review *Lacerba* (founded by Giovanni Papini and Ardengo Soffici), which would then be the most important of those associated with Marrinetti's movement and in which a poet of the importance of Giuseppe Ungaretti would publish his first poems.

Around this time the famous "futurist evenings" began, the main aim of which was scandalize the bourgeois public, and which gave rise to continuous provocations and dramatic episodes which ended, as often as not, in real brawls. (The shows were composed of declamations, genuine invective, screamed recitations, rhythmic improvisations).

But what were the fundamental principles of futurist poetry? A great Italian critic, Gianfranco Contini, has offered the most effective synthetic definition: "the term 'futurism' is opposed to 'pastism' and posits a separation from rational tradition, the classic, the academic and also the sentimental ("Let us kill off the light of the moon!", is the title of one of Marinetti's lampoons), and the foundation of a new mythology taken from the contemporary world of technology and speed: an appropriate symbol of this technological, violent and reckless attitude is the substitution, suggested in the first manifesto, of the racing car (the term was then freshly coined) for the *Victory of Samothrace* as a standard of beauty. The fundamental canon of futurism is simultaneity between impression and expression, put into effect in literature by means of the slogan "words in freedom": freedom from conventional rhythms, from grammatical conventions, developing to the limit an onomatopoeic capacity which goes right to the heart of articulated speech, that ought to contract – in order to represent the synergism of several orders of feelings and the rapidity of passages – to a series of nouns juxtaposed without punctuation and modulated with typographical innovations. As one can see, the result is a total overthrow not only of traditional poetry and rhetoric but also of grammatical speech itself, resulting in the foundation of a sort of anti-speech that became the ambiguous standard bearer of those who claimed it to represent the most authentic and revolutionary energies of the new Italian youth. Unavoidably, the more recognized national poetic tradition, that had in such figures as Carducci and Pascoli two unavoidable points of reference, hotly contested all this and detached themselves from the myth of the so-called "new man", who could even arrive at an unconditioned approval of the great war that was looming on the horizon, or could look too kindly on the rise of the great industrial monopolies who would shortly come to affirm Mussolini and the consolidation of the fascist regime.

It goes without saying that the youthful anti-bourgeois rebellion of the futurists, although lacking in any rigorous ideologically-aware foundation, was characterized by a paradoxical blend of innovation and conservatism, of creative impulse and destruction, revolution and acceptance. Also the admiration directed towards the world of industry and technology completely lacked any critical quality and was entirely focussed on its external and more spectacular aspects, on the huge and showy surface of mechanization and technical progress. Moreover, Italian literary futurism does not include many remarkable personalities, and the innovation of the programme and the collective impetus of the generational group, the spirit and innovation of the movement would soon turn out to be more important and interesting than the individuals who comprised it. It is always the movement that precedes the individual personalities that join them, and futurism first of all remains important for this collective impulse, for this unanimity of poetic action, for the subversive intention that sustains it. It goes without saying that the program laid out in the *Technical Manifesto of Futurist Literature*, which would be published in Italian as it was in French in 1912, contains in itself the same constructive and communicative limits that will always constrain futurist poetry in some orthodox measure to the original dictates of the movement and that it consists in the same anti-discursive nature of the "words in freedom" notion: the destruction of syntax (obviously an affinity with the new organization of space proposed by cubist painting), verbs in the infinitive, abolition of the adjective, the adverb and punctuation, the use of more and more immense analogies (this last point reveals a not insignificant link between Marinetti and French symbolist poetry and in particular with the poetics of *correspondances* of Baudelaire and the free analogic system of Rimbaud).

In particular, in the eleventh point of the Manifesto Marinetti gives a precise indication and one of great significance: "To destroy the 'I' in literature, that is the whole psychology. The man completely damaged by the library and the museum, in thrall to logic and a fearful wisdom, is of absolutely no interest any more. Therefore, we must abolish it in literature, and replace it finally with material, the essence of which is to be seized by violent intuition, the one thing which the physicist and chemist will never be able to make". The consequence of this attitude that was proposed as a polemical gesture against the entire European tradition of psychological realism, was the exaltation of the moment immediately and unconsciously perceived of so-called external truth, but which would end – the other contradiction of Italian literary futurism – in a sort of passive and a sterile recording of phenomena (the critic Glauco Viazzi has written: "In *paroliberas**, futurist writing works as a gestural method of 'active' recording of a phenomenology that includes both bodily and psychic expressions as well as material factuality". From this point of view we are surely dealing with important intuitions that, if they do not come to fruition in the ambit of Italian literary futurism, can be found in the absolute values attained by other more successful and better-known stylistic revolutions. In particular, dadaism and surrealism would come to inherit by no means insignificant elements of the work on language and deep impersonality carried out by Marinetti and his colleagues (as would, it should be added, the poetic output of remarkable personalities such as Apollinaire and Mayakovsky). As far as Italy goes, that means the great poetry of Ungaretti, in *Porto sepolto* and then in *Allegria*, which refined and worked through the radically innovative suggestions of the futurist program, succeeding in some measure to use some of those techniques for the foundation of a poetic speech of depth and of absolute value (a critic of the importance of Luciano Anceschi has asserted that it was Ungaretti himself who collected and made fruitful much that the futurists had achieved in the destruction of traditional poetic language without coming to an equally successful and effective reconstruction). The important results of futurism were achieved only outside poetry and in particular in the realm of figurative art. In fact they were accepted or were felt in varied measure by the finest artists such as Giorgio Morandi, Ottone Rosai, but above all Carl Carrà and the brilliant Umberto Boccioni, killed in combat in 1916, who has left probably the most representative sculpture and painting of the time. Moreover, as Fausto Curi, an important and acute student of futurism and Modernist European poetry, has written, "one of the most revolutionary inventions in *Ulysses* and *Finnegans Wake*, that is the inner monologue, while it is or it seems close to the technique of mimesis and to the oral flow realized in *paroliberas* texts, derived from Marinetti's overthrowing of relevance and late naturalism". In fact, as Curi also maintains, Marinetti's *Zang Tumb Tumb* can be considered as "an uninterrupted, screamed interior monologue". Coming back then to Italy, one can say that the resonant, strident hostility towards the Italian poetic tradition exhibited by the futurists resulted

> Your objections? All right! I know them! Of course! We know just what our beautiful false intelligence affirms: "We are only the sum and the prolongation of our ancestors", it says. Perhaps! All right! What does it matter? But we will not listen! Take care not to repeat those infamous words! Instead, lift up your head! Standing on the world's summit we launch once again our insolent challenge to the stars!
> Filippo Marinetti,
> *The Futurist Manifesto*

---

*A form of art in which visual and verbal experiences are closely combined.

in the so-called "return to order" that distinguishes the poetic experiences of the first post-war period: from the more specifically classicist programme associated with Vincenzo Cardarelli and the re-united writers of the review *Ronda*, to the new formal reconstruction produced by Ungaretti in *Sentimento del tempo* (the rehabilitation, after the breathtaking experience of absolute language, of the hendecasyllabic and seven-syllable lines of noble literary ancestry), to the nihilistic and metaphysical existentialism, of great objective firmness, of Eugenio Montale, resulting in the construction of a *Canzoniere* poetic of explicit autobiographical nature on the part of Umberto Saba.

If we analyze the course of Italian narrative in the passage from the nineteenth to the twentieth century and in particular the novels and theatre of Luigi Pirandello (in some measure a theatre of ambiguity anticipating Artaud) and of Joyce's disciple Italo Svevo, in which the trace of the psychological and individual "I" tends to become more and more evanescent and vanishes, to flow into, in Svevo's *Cosciena di Zeno*, an authentic dissolution and untenability of the biographical figure, it becomes apparent that Marinetti's intuitions belong in the path, if not to the apex, of a such process of attacking the institutions (in an anthropological sense) of the bourgeois system. From this point of view, the proposals of the Futurist Manifesto appear, in their programmatic and simplified exhortations, not at all abstract but, on the contrary, they become an extreme, paradoxical and, all considered, impossible attempt at realism and absolute objectification, almost to the point not just of depriving the language of its traditional poetic content, but of ending in total and irredeemable impersonality. In their antilogical and antirational polemic and in their hostility towards the material and the elementary, their game of free combinations of various elements, the futurists were aiming for a language that possessed the luminous splendour of metal and the lightning speed of a locomotive, resulting in, as between things, a total consistency and material integrity (relevant here is the importance attributed to the iconic values of poetic compositions, the disposition of the written text and the manipulation of its graphical characters, to the point that in futurist poetry the borders between literature and visual art becomes much more uncertain and hazy compared to a traditional text). So also in poetics, Marinetti's "words in freedom" (which are somewhat anticipated in the experimental free verse of Piero Lucini) take their place within a wider reaction and answer to the crisis of the naturalistic and symbolist tradition, which after the pomp of the 1900s, appeared almost to have expired in an inert and predictable classicism.

Besides Marinetti and the orthodox futurists, we should mention the work of some lesser known avant-garde artists: Corrado Govoni, Aldo Palazzeschi (whose beginnings are ascribed to the futurism), the previously cited Ungaretti and also Dino Campana, a nocturnal and visionary poet in whom musical fascination exceeds and transforms the direct referentiality of poetic speech.

Finally the lessons of futurism in Italy have been used again and revalued in Italy also in the inner contradictions of the neo-vanguard of the second half of the century, represented first of all by the *novisssimi* poets (Sanguineti, Giuliani, Balestrini, Pagliarani, Porta) and taken further by the ferocious team of the "group '63". The futurism of the Neo-avant-garde has taken up again (trimmed this time to fit within an avowedly Marxist ideological and avant-garde interpretative system), the cohesion of the movement, the prevalence of poetic theory (without doubt more interesting than the poetic texts) and above all the original intuition of the anti-demystificatory polemic that the futurist poets levelled against bourgeois institutionalised language and its instrumental and intimidating value.

Translated from the Italian by Peter Forbes

THE WAY OF THE POET
A weekend residential workshop in Sussex
28/29 August 1999

led by
GRACE NICHOLS
Nationally and Internationally
well-known Caribbean poet
and
BARBARA COLE
Transpersonal Psychotherapist
Consultant and Trainer

Two days of self discovery and creativity in the inspiring Sussex countryside. Open to anybody who wants to take a deeper look at themselves, open up to their creativity, look at what blocks it, and express themselves in poetry.

Enquiries/Bookings to:
Barbara Cole, 4 Offham Terrace, Lewes,
East Sussex BN7 2QP
Tel/Fax: 01273 473113

MAURIZIO CUCCHI
THE WOOD ON THE ISLAND

I am no longer in my own home,
but in this airy place which allows me everything.
Its peaceful geometry
is an entrance to clarity for the damp, light
bodies on the balcony
in the holiday tracks of slothful indifference.

I listen from here to the voices in the piazza,
and study like a lake the sea that opens
in the wood and if there's wind
a domestic countryside of cicadas
which at midday protects our steps
when time no longer has direction:

on the whole flat deserted plain
and on the frontier cut in lengths, which is misting over.

*

Fritz had told me rather out of the corner of his mouth
that there was night life on the island.
I thought of those little steep places,
and labyrinths, of those slim trunks, of getting bogged down
alone in the darkness and tasting
the unnecessary panic, the lost feeling, the shivers,
the earth.
I had to go back to childhood images from Alpine foothills,
to cyclamens, to dampness, to smells and scents,
in order to get myself too
in there between the lovely paths covered with night.
But those fellows who came and knocked,
in the dark hours of wind and storm,
at our little house and woke us up,
had less grand mysteries in their shoes
and so the thick dark would have chewed them up
or else some grass snake in the silence
would have come and gently rubbed against them.

*

We are all individuals, distinct
like the stones in a cobbled street.

I am a flask, a bladder
and I sweat out me from my own inner being.

*

Holidays open for us a sweet void
with everything left hanging and at departure
they stir us and breathe away as if endless.

I love the people of the month of August,
who float on the surface of the air
and in time that is half-asleep.
I love the crowd that has no names,
quietly exploring the avenues
and laughing at the sea in open-air cafes.

Wearing my awful hat,
I'm already here waiting for the bus.
I keep turning to look back,
I've got my eyes on the slope,
but in the meantime the island has disappeared.

Translated by Alistair Elliot

CLAUDIO DAMIANI
ALBIO'S THE SMALL NUT-TREE ON THE LEFT

Albio's the small nut-tree on the left
of the road as you go up it from the house
towards the gate. As I went past this morning
I looked at him and saw he'd given birth
to little walnuts, pairs of them, already
quite big, a glossy green, a little sparse,
not that many but lovely ones and I thought
the year before he hadn't yet produced
at all, and this year was his first time ever
for having them, and then I looked as well

at his leaves: bright, perfect, oval,
without one single blemish, not one spot
or puncture at all; and also at the small branches
high up down to the slim and shiny trunk
quite white, and at the perfect gentle shape
of the whole little tree standing up straight
in the light there, and I thought that all around
the appletrees, the pear, the plum, the two
poor little cypresses bent by the snow,
the roses, even, to be perfectly frank, the weeds
have some disease and you are just so healthy
by contrast, glossy, beautiful and clean
Albio, standing firm in your sweet nook
in the light there; and I thought (and it seemed to me
you stood as if you were expecting somebody
or something), I thought and thought: they all have something
wrong with them, there's not one with nothing wrong
at all, and yes I should I really should
have treated them, administered poisons, pruned
their branches and I haven't done a thing,
on top of which I'm going to have to leave
the house and all this soon: the two small cypresses
and Antenor, always first in the apple-orchard
to bloom, and the fig and little fir, both dead
and the roses and the wild grass that grows back

without a break and my love's garden too
all this I shall have to leave, all this, and you
Albio are so lovely, why oh why
are you so healthy and so lovely Albio?
for whom? I thought, for whom? . . . I could almost hear
his glad and quiet breath and then a shadow
stooping and in the light a brightness
I was already chasing off, I didn't want
to see it, I was going back already
along the road and didn't know your glory
I didn't know it, or know anything,
and then into my eyes the tears came.

Translated by Alistair Elliot

ANDREA GIBELLINI
MY CITY

My city is not a city
it has its life between the river and the country
it's hung up near the hills
and if you dig there you can uncover
fish that come from the past
carved in the limestone;
the blue of the sky like the sea is only dreamed
in the silence, under the white of the stone
and the few clumps of flowers.
The boughs of trees that are no longer trees

go down to touch the river
batter against the boulders, break
the chill waters troubled by silence –
far off the Secchia flows away in the dark –
but it's the vision of a young river,
long gone.

City in winter

shut in the mist
waiting for the prettier season
in the sun of spring
(a strange field of a violet blue
that they cut in fan shapes
against a new white block of flats
and the smoke from potteries
rising like natural summer clouds...)
that today at last I see and don't remember.

The flowers shut in between old walls,
dried up grasses
the strong smell of the river, –
beside me as always
a beloved voice,
the winged fish hidden in the limestone
the grey everlasting mud, over the rocks,
from delicate mosses that have blown away.

The piazza is an oblong under a charm
(from high up, where the green is,
coming down towards the city...)

the gravel-covered field – pierced by a courtyard.

And the sadness is sweet –

like the air in the morning
between the houses
of a far-off summer.

I don't and I wouldn't want to be my city

– and whether I think it or not
my blood flows
through those caves in the clay –
but too close and too like me

is the beating

the coldness of the useless heart.

Translated by Alistair Elliot

THREE POEMS BY DAVIDE RONDONI
PREGNANT SAYS THE TEST

Don't call him, he's coming
full of his near-translucent strength,
already he's a part of your smile
he comes like the scent from the woods,
a nothing with the unforeseen snout
of a hare, he is already a fold
in your hands, he sits
on the throne you're turning into.

        He is a growth
with an excess of clouds,
he's frightening like the starting-up of a wind
that bends the branches but revives the colours.
My love, beautiful and full of worry,
his mark is there already on our
shape. Happiness
is waiting, happiness is time.

BARTOLOMEO

When you too stop in this great
motorway caff and see
your own exhausted face run
on the windows, on the aluminium counter,

it'll be an evening like this
that breaks up in wind the light
and clouds of the day, it'll be
a great moment:
only you and I will know.

                    You will set off again
slightly upset, with almost a stir
of memory and the separate silences
of the shelves of objects, the petrolpump men and their caps,
you'll feel behind you nimbly
becoming a poem.

The happiness of time is saying yes
you are there, a hidden power
gives you a shock, not my
youth which is going, not my
maturity, not my growing old –
the real likeness between us
is in a place where it can't be seen.

My son, my traveller,
it's going to be your hell, your talent
this sense of hearing like a dog's or angel's
which picks up as one tune the swing of the planets
and the fall of a pill in a glass
two storeys down, where two old people
are being cared for.
This very noisy love
will be your father, the real one.

Stay longer here in the motorway caff,
it'll please me in the dark to see you again...

TO GIUSEPPE UNGARETTI,
SEEN AT NIGHT ON TV READING 'RIVERS'

I don't, myself, have rivers,
I've never lived leaning out
with my face over the water
that still or eddying round
carves through the city, ennobles or in whirls
steals away all its thoughts.
                          I've not had
flights of wide stone steps on which to lie stretched out
losing under the sunshine
the light of the intellect, dozing off.
                             I had avenues,
streets broad and full of noise, the high trajectory
of slip-roads,
those open arms of a mother who is poor
veins by which every kind of stuff
comes into town.
I have had avenues of trees
or blasts of vertigo between the steel of walls
and darkened glass.
                    The confusion
makes them identical, under the rain
they amount to hell,
              frenzy.
                      But at night, when night
does fall
they are drawn again,
                  fresh avenues
of shade and loneliness,
when the drooping necks of lamp-posts
light them up and the switching off
of the last advertisement signs.
They begin to move then, very lightly,
they branch out, perhaps the whole city
rotates a little;
                somebody ends up
face to face with a castle or a
cathedral, others lose their tan
under the orange lamps of a motorway junction –
the avenues at night breathe
with the leaves of plane-trees, broad black fans,

with the grilles of the underground and the lullaby air
that sleeps over children.
                        They draw breath when
the passenger of the last tram goes –
                              The avenues give me
a special life
which is not tears and joy,
no, but a windy emptiness,
                    a sense of going
going on and on
that comes to me from who knows what seas,
what valleys, what great rivers.

Translated by Alistair Elliott

VALERIO MAGRELLI

    And the crack in the teacup opens
    A lane to the land of the dead.
    (W. H. Auden)

    as when a crack appears
    the length of a cup.
    (R. M. Rilke)

You gave me this red cup
from which to drink to my days on earth
one by one
in the pallid mornings, the pearls
strung on thirst's long necklace.
And should it fall and crack,
stunned by regret
I'll have to mend it
so as to keep unbroken
that sequence of kisses.
And each time the round
of handle or rim
chips, I'll glue it back
together until
my love has finished
the slow hard graft of a mosaic.

Right down the dip of the cup's white slope,
along the clear curved inside,
like a jag of lightning,
fixed and black,
the crack descends
– sign of a storm
whose thunder still echoes
over this landscape
of glazed resonance.

Translated by Jamie McKendrick

Crackling Firework

by Peter Forbes

EUGENIO MONTALE
Collected Poems 1920-1954
Carcanet, £29
ISBN 1 857544 25 0

NEW TRANSLATIONS OF Montale have appeared regularly since his death, but Galassi's book is the most sumptuous. It is far from being a *Complete Poems*, ending in 1954 with four more books to come. Galassi justifies his choice thus: "Montale's later poetry, written in his sixties, seventies, and eighties, is largely an ironic commentary on what went before…a second and secondary body of work".

Montale's sensibility is an acquired taste. His world can seem claustrophobic, his poems *paysages moralisés* in which the landscape about which the myths are woven – the Ligurian coast – is bleached, harsh, a tangle of erosion and detritus. Much of the poetry exploits the conventional desolation of objects: "My life is this dry slope, / A means not an end, a way / Open to runoffs from gutter and slow erosions. / And it's this too: this plant / Born out of devastation / That takes the sea's lashing in the face".

His imagery throughout tends towards the astringent, the pungent, the winnowed: "the copper horizon", "Acid knot of suffocated notes", "parched by salt sea wind", "rabid sirocco / gale".

As with Rilke, nothing much happens in Montale's poems. He describes himself, in the 'Mediterranean' section of *Cuttlefish Bones*, as "a brooding man / who sees the turbulence of fleeting life / in himself, in others – who's slow to take / the action no one can later undo". It is antipastoral, in which objects are lovingly described although the emotion they evoke is sterile. The recent poet closest to him is Walcott, especially in *Midsummer*.

This is a bilingual edition, which anyone with a little Italian will find useful, but beware: his vocabulary is as broad as his subject is narrow. The intoxication of Montale's language was well caught in Jeremy Reed's versions of 1991 in *The Coastguard's House* (Bloodaxe). Reed took some liberties but his recreations (inspired by Lowell's in *Imitations*) seemed true to the spirit. Galassi is generally more accurate, but not always. In Galassi's version, the great poem 'News from Mount Amiata' begins: "The stormy weather's fireworks / Will be a murmur of beehives by late evening". Reed has: "The crackling firework of sultry weather / Turns to a beehive simmer of thunder". Reed's is far superior, having a rhythm where the Galassi is flat; it also in this case actually mirrors the original more closely. The other important translations these versions have to contend with are William Arrowsmith's, versions which I still slightly prefer. The problem with new translations for an old reader is that, like a favoured interpretation of great piece of music, or the Bible, the early version is simply the form by which the work became known to us, and thus has a hard-to-unlearn primal authority. The only solution, in the end, is to learn the language. Despite these caveats, Galassi's is a fine edition, and is likely to be the one through which new readers will encounter Montale.

Petersburgers

CAROL RUMENS ON THE CONVERSATION OF "POETRY'S LATTERDAY PROPHET"

SOLOMON VOLKOV
Conversations with Joseph Brodsky
The Free Press (Simon & Schuster), £17.99
ISBN 0 684 83572 X

IN THE AUTUMN of 1978, Solomon Volkov, then still a newish émigré to the USA, went along to Columbia University to hear Joseph Brodsky lecture: he was impressed, and approached the poet afterwards with the astute notion of collaborating on a book of "conversations that would explore poetry and Russian culture through the lens of his experience". Brodsky's response was positive, a fact which surprised Volkov at the time. Later, he understood. Brodsky was only thirty-six but soon to undergo his first bout of cardiac surgery. He would have known that a possible death-sentence impended.

The two began meeting in Brodsky's apartment, and the result of their "sometimes heated" conversations is this baggy, exciting, unpredictable and occasionally maddening book. To begin with the most serious quibble: whatever Volkov's initial scheme, the result is a hybrid, its purpose not only to induct Brodsky's thoughts on poetry and culture but to give us a Brodsky "life". The chapters on the poet's earlier experiences tend, therefore, to throw up the following kind of "conversation":

> **Brodsky** (describing his cell in the Leningrad "Big House"): What was in it? A bedside table, a sink and an *ochko*. What else?
> **Volkov**: What's an *ochko*?
> **Brodsky**: An *ochko*? It's a hole in the floor, it's the toilet. I don't understand. Where were you?

On such occasions it's better to skip Volkov's seemingly disingenuous interventions. Brodsky's narrative does not belong to the conversational genre, and perhaps he should have simply been given his own monologue, at least in the edited transcript (I accept that he may have needed some prompting from Volkov during the original conversation). The narrative itself of course, is compelling – both as a portrait of a political and artistic period low and dishonest far beyond Auden's or any English writer's experience, and as a complex self-portrait. Brodsky describes his experiences as vividly as if they had occurred yesterday, with a scathing vigour, a total absence of self-pity and a fine sense of the absurd. Volkov cannot very well compare notes: his answer to Brodsky's question, where were you? is that he was studying music at the Leningrad Conservatory. Later on, he left Russia, with the usual bureaucratic difficulty, but without the trauma of Brodsky's involuntary dispatch. His experiences would nevertheless have made an interesting contrast and additional perspective. But that, no doubt, would have been incompatible with the publisher's marketing strategy, inappropriate for the general reader of the Brodsky "life". It is for this reader, I presume, that those insultingly banal endnotes are intended ("Chaliapin: mighty Russian bass: Cavafy: great Greek poet", etc.).

When the two Petersburgers converse as equals, the book takes off, and the genre proves its unique value, Volkov is fluent, confident, witty and highly knowledgeable about literature: he frequently gives as good as he gets: see, for example, the discussion on Marina Tsvetaeva ("Russian poet who Brodsky often claimed was the greatest of the twentieth-century" etc.):

> **Volkov**: I don't like Tsvetaeva's pointing finger, her eagerness to chew everything up and regurgitate a rhymed prescriptive truth that may not have been worth the hiss.
> **Brodsky**: Nonsense! There's nothing like that in Tsvetaeva. There is a thought – as a rule, an extremely uncomfortable thought – taken to its conclusion. Hence, perhaps, your impression that this thought is wagging its finger at you, so to speak. One can speak of a certain preachiness with respect to Pasternak – "Living a life is not crossing a field" – and so forth, but definitely not Tsvetaeva. If the content of Tsvetaeva's poetry could be reduced to some formula, then it's this: "To your insane world! But one reply — I refuse". And Tsvetaeva actually derives a certain satisfaction from this refusal, She says no with a palpable satisfaction: *ny-e-t!*
> **Volkov**: Tsvetaeva has an aphoristic quality. She can be pilfered quote by quote, almost like Griboedov's

Woe from Wit.
Brodsky: Oh, definitely!
Volkov: But for some reason this aphoristic quality has always repelled me.

And so it goes on, until the combatants agree to differ, and the discussion ranges off in new directions, via a brief skirmish in the territory of Women's Writing: "**Volkov**: Does a woman's voice in poetry really not differ in any way from a man's? **Brodsky**: Only in the verb-endings". Nice one, Joseph.

Some of the conversations show Brodsky trying out the ideas that he will later refine in his marvellous prose essays. Perhaps the discursiveness of the conversational medium actually helped him make discoveries in his thinking. To read these transcripts is almost to see a cross-section of human brains in action, sparking ideas across the synapses, laying down new connective tissue. The Tsvetaeva passage quoted above graphically illustrates how ideas can give birth to other ideas, even if only in their own self-defence. Two good minds really can get farther than one.

Volkov, of course, is ultimately respectful: the poet always has his say. The conversational genre suits an intellect like Brodsky's because it allows him to improvise, to bring into play his extraordinary eclecticism. He can afford to be irrelevant. Talking about Frost, for example, he floats broad questions which would waste time in the American Poetry seminar but which instantly light up several areas: how is Frost like his Russian contemporaries, how is he utterly different from them? Brodsky forges his poetics from elements that do not naturally coalesce: Akhmatova and Frost, Tsvetaeva and Auden, the Silver Age and the age of the MacPoem (to borrow Donald Hall's memorable term). Perhaps he can best be understood as a latecomer to Modernism, a movement whose poets might be seen as the true heirs to the Acmeists and their famous "nostalgia for world culture". Intellectually, he is closest of all to Eliot, the American who went to England and made his poems from a wide range of unlikely connections – Jacobean tragedy and French Symbolism, Lewis Carroll and the Book of Common Prayer. Modernism in Europe and the USA may have had its moment (like the Chinese stir-fry it resembles, its moment is brief) but, in Russia, perhaps, the magical dish has just arrived. What is interesting about Brodsky's Modernism is, of course, that it contains some very old-fashioned ingredients. The poet is nostalgic for stanza-form as well as world culture and he argues brilliantly for that tradition which packs its poetry in salt. American formalism is back in town, of course: perhaps Brodsky was the one who smuggled it in. No-one else, surely, would dare to talk about *belles lettres*, let alone succeed in restoring the term's faded glory. His view of poetry matters, particularly to us in the West, because he is innocent enough to know what "good poetry" is – not only in his own language and culture but in ours – a culture which often does not know, and does not want to know, such things.

He can be "silly like us", too, of course, and it is sometimes difficult to decide when brilliant becomes batty. "The poet's role in society is to animate it – the people no less than the furniture" (perhaps he had accidentally tipped over a chair as he was speaking?). The Moskovskaya vodka logo is "a hieroglyph for infinity"(why not – specially after half a bottle?). But when he informs us happily that "The lyrics of 'Yellow Submarine' are perfectly marvellous… the best examples of the English and American light verse genre… what is there to say? Even Brodsky can get it wrong sometimes. On other occasions it is the translation that is number-one suspect. For example, the duo have a discussion about Akhmatova's "religiosity" when surely they are simply discussing her religious faith. Gennadi Smakov, the homosexual ballet critic, upset by gibes about his name, must have changed it *to*, rather than *from*, Shmakov. A malevolent critic accuses Brodsky of "climbing to fame over the steps of the Russian language". This doesn't sound to me like much of an insult, and I suspect misquotation, at least. However, these are minor gripes: Marian Schwarz has produced a translation of such natural-sounding colloquialism and vigour that it's only rarely we remember that the original combatants were sparring in quite a different language.

There is debate, not all of it ill-intentioned, about how great a poet Brodsky really was. But in fact it wouldn't matter if he turned out to be the worst poet of the century: by talking about poetry in the way he does, he still shows us what great poetry is. It's a peculiar talent. Poets are not expected to be poets except on the pages of their work. Brodsky is a poet in his daily self, his moral attitudes, and hence in his conversation – which works very much as a poem does with its leaping connective flashes. He is not poetry's PR man: there are plenty of those around. He is more than a brilliant critic. Somehow or other this self-taught maverick, this homely idealist and hero-worshipper and opener of mental windows, turned himself into poetry's latterday prophet. Telling Volkov how he dared to become a teacher of American (and English) poetry to Americans, he explains that "poetic texts are precious – more precious... because my life – to say nothing of my world-view – was changed by these texts". And, elsewhere: "These people simply created us – Frost, Tsvetaeva, Cavafy, Rilke, Akhmatova, Pasternak". Brodsky, it seems, did not just read the poetry but submitted himself to being read by it.

The person who emerges from this book is one who has the grandest view of poetry and yet the most generous. He asks us to read Krilov and Derjhavin as well as Pushkin and Mandelstam: "poetry requires more than just one master of minds". He manages to be democratic without cheapening the aesthetic, to be reverend without piety, and to make judgements without personal cruelty. And the moral qualities – the bravery under persecution, the generosity to his friends and students, might persuade us there was sense in Leavis after all: that aesthetic and ethical values are in some way interdependent and, in some personalities at least, can act as mutual guarantors. Anyone disturbed by the recent horrible spectacle of shite-chucking at the new Poet Laureate is advised to spend a few healing hours in this book. To stop reading, though, is to remember that the voice ran out of breath many years too soon. I did not know Brodsky well, but he felt like a friend, and I think for anyone who cared about poetry, even if they had never met him, this would have been true. We must go into the twenty-first century without him, a frightening prospect. Don't go, at least, without this book.

TWO POEMS BY ALLA GELICH
THE ROOM

I remember the room, that room in a government office.
Three gleaming tables branched like a white gallows.
I sit before them there, a tailor's dummy,
Endlessly repeating, as in a dream:

I didn't ask for details.
Didn't see. Don't know the date.
The light grows dimmer with the close of day,
And, drop by drop, life seeps out of me.

My temples pound. Darkness through the window.
Shall I move a bit? Whisper for water maybe?
No, it's too late . . . Again those monotonous tones,
Bespectacled eyes swim at me out of darkness.

THE CHAIR

The electric chair
Need not be wired,
Execution
Can dispense with a switch.
You can finish a man
According to schedule,
Whenever you wish,
In an ordinary chair.

What a pleasure to watch
The trembling hands,
Hear the light roll
Of chattering teeth.
It's good to have learned
The right technique
For the one in the chair
(They once used a stake).
You're trembling, my dear.
Did you get a touch?
If you don't hold tight
You'll fall from your chair.

All over our capital
The sentence of death
Is carried out
In ordinary chairs.

Translated from the Russian by Antony Wood

Author's note: 'The Room' and 'The Chair' were written in 1973, each one after the event: 'The Room' after her first interrogation at the KGB headquarters; 'The Chair' – after the most strenuous of subsequent interrogations. The full story of completely unexpected arrest and detention, then house search, interrogations and fight for one's sanity, followed by even more unexpected victory and escape to the free world is described in her short story 'Poetry Workshop, Lubyanka Street' in which these poems are included.

EUGENE DUBNOV
I MAKE MY WAY TO THE EMPTY HOUSE

In memory of Nina Bein

I make my way to the empty house:
Once, in there, children laughed and cried.
So I face the past: the place
Where the living died.

She stands there again at the window
High, on that upper floor,
Telling the children "Now don't you go
Too far off" – as so often before –

And I'm stopped: the beat
Of a footfall would be too rude:
They'd be too light, these feet
For such heavy solitude.

Translated from the Russian by Herbert Lomas with the author.

Voices for Kosovo

Produced in association with the charity Children's Aid Direct, this anthology aims to raise awareness and – more importantly – money for the refugee crisis in Kosovo. It is an anthology to challenge, inform and stimulate the reader, one that will save lives.

Contributors include those involved in the situation, either as victims of war or as aid workers, and a selection of writing by famous and not-so-famous authors from all over the British Isles and beyond.

All money from sales of this book is going to Children's Aid Direct. Please order this book.

£7.50 per copy, post free, from
Stride, 11 Sylvan Road, Exeter, Devon EX4 6EW
(cheques payable to 'Stride')

REVIEWS

The Melancholic Monkey

ANDREW ZAWACKI ON THE PROTEAN APPETITE OF TOMAZ SALAMUN

TOMAZ SALAMUN
The Four Questions of Melancholy: New and Selected Poems
Ed. Christopher Merrill
White Pine, $15.00.
ISBN 1 877727 57 1

ENGLISH-SPEAKING READERS, if they know the work of Slovenian poet Tomaz Salamun at all, will have read it in his Ecco Press selection of 1988, edited by Charles Simic and introduced by Robert Hass. *The Four Questions of Melancholy: New and Selected Poems*, the first volume in the new Terra Incognita series established by White Pine Press, makes available to the West three times as much of ˇalamun's poetry. Editor Christopher Merrill's short introduction to Salamun's life and its relationship to the dynamics of political change in the former Yugoslavia is indispensable, and it also helps in situating Salamun's poetry in the context of European and American letters. Drawing from Salamun's twenty-five collections, beginning with *Poker* (1966) and concluding with *Ambergris* (1994), and representing the work of thirteen translators, *The Four Questions of Melancholy* is a testament to three decades of writing by one of Central Europe's leading voices.

Salamun was born in Croatia in 1941. As the young editor of Perspektive, Yugoslavia's leading political and cultural monthly, he was imprisoned for five days by the Communist authorities who had banned its publication. The notoriety did nothing to harm Salamun's fledgling poetry career, however, and he proceeded to take an M. A. in art history at the University of Ljubljana and to exhibit his conceptual art at the Museum of Modern Art in 1970. Two years later, he enrolled in the International Writing Program at the University of Iowa and subsequently took up residencies at both the Yaddo and McDowell writing colonies. He is currently the cultural attache to the Consulate General of Slovenia in New York, a city whose poets, especially Frank O'Hara and John Ashbery, have been integral to Salamun's development and maturity.

Robert Hass has argued that while the generation preceding Salamun's – Vasko Popa, Miroslav Holub, Zbigniew Herbert – had assumed a defiant stance to the state, manifesting itself in anti-Communist allegories and fables, Salamun helped to usher in a new, less overtly political poetics. Poetry for Salamun's generation was beginning to return to its visionary, spiritual roots, and however much Salamun has ironized himself and the whole notion of finding some sort of transcendence in that slippery, playful thing called language, he has nonetheless persevered in approaching a divine fulfilment:

> I live for this: to sink in the sun
> to gaze at light like the level sea
> to see the dust and us the dust a field
> in eyes the lord's footsteps, a velvet silence...

"Poetry is a parallel process to spiritual development", he has said: "You are trained how to be with the world as long as you can endure it".

Salamun's poetry is indeed of the world, and he has been informed by international poetry in the most comprehensive sense: "Salamun's tradition has been the disruptive, visionary side of European experimental art", argues Hass, "Rimbaud, Lautréamont, the German expressionists, the French surrealists, the Russian futurists". Merrill writes of the present selection, "Here are surrealist lists, Whitmanic catalogues, sonnets, New York School-style improvisations". Add to that list the L=A=N=G=U=A=G=E poetry of Clark Coolidge, Ray DiPalma and Tom Raworth, the mythic consciousness of Octavio Paz and the Latin American tradition of negativity, the lyric ephemerality of Eugenio Montale and other heirs to Leopardi, Old Testament portents and psalmic litanies, Laforgue's precociousness, and a vaguely Beat vernacular. This is to say nothing of the Slovenian poetic heritage out of which Salamun has grown, even while having radically ruptured it. In 'To Edvard Kocbek on His 70th Birthday', Salamun commemorates Slovenia's most important twentieth-century poet by admitting an anxiety of influence:

I have avoided you, great poet
and thinker, you were too heavy
a burden. I drew a fierce line behind me
so that I would be at ease, light...

Salamun credits Kocbek with being, "more than anyone... the shaper / of our freedom", concluding that even under the shadow of Kocbek, or perhaps because of his presence, "Moment / by moment joy strengthens". Salamun himself has become that great poet, ministering to an accomplished band of successors in Slovenia, foremost among them the poet and social critic Ales Debeljak, author of the widely-acclaimed *Anxious Moments* (White Pine, 1994) and the Terra Incognita series general editor. What budding reputation Slovenian poets – whose first language is only spoken by two million – have in America is largely due to Salamun's example.

It is a kind of strengthening joy that Salamun has always proffered, even though, as he says beautifully of Versailles in the sonnet of that name, "You are Slovenian, therefore sad". Salamun's poetry gives the impression that melancholy is always a condition of aesthetics and living, with joy its somewhat hermetic half-brother. Nonetheless, Salamun has mastered the hide-and-seek of irony, often cloaking the Eastern European despair which Milan Kundera calls *litost* behind playfulness and spontaneity. "I keep on laughing / or am melancholic as a monkey", he writes. But how melancholic is a monkey? Salamun's four questions of melancholy are, first and foremost, questions, and as Merrill observes, they go unanswered in Rilke's spirit of loving questions for their own revelatory sake:

Where is your rabbit?
What's in the backpack? Why are you chewing straw?
And why so sad? Shadows have consumed the valley
now, and the last train has hobbled off to Bohinj.

The poem ends in questions, too, an ironic counterpoint to the opening assertion, "I know. You're off to war now"... His sort-of pastoral is evasive, the "you" never named, his rabbit never explained, the cause for sadness also left unknown, and shadows encroaching. The poem acts as a mythology by itself, mythology being the manner in which humanity has attempted to characterize the unintelligible. In the end the explanations themselves are more compelling than the actual phenomena behind them.

But Salamun is not a mere mythmaker in the tradition of so many contemporary Orphei. What initially set him apart from his Eastern European forebears was his quizzical technique of self-mythologizing. His Whitmanic world-unto-himself is remarkable for the immense space it allows to range from an extreme negative capability to its obverse of self-realization or self-actualization. By creating myths of and for himself, Salamun can be at once chameleonic, inhabiting the forms of everything under the sun by means of a radical otherness, as well as quasi-mystical, divesting what's around him and leaving only his true self in the husk of the world. Over the course of his career he has affected reincarnation to its most sublime, ridiculous degree:

I am the people's point of view, a cow,
the tropical wind, I sleep under the surface.
I am the aristocratic carnivore, I eat form.....

More people will see me, with sunrise I become
morning.

There are not enough things in the world for the protean Salamun: he becomes a rooster, then a roe, a cactus, a stone, the bottom of pain, a train, hay, smoke, and everything from "such a Mediterranean rock I you can broil steak on me" to "dew in a can which I a child can carry, / I am sweet white milk". The real Salamun is both humorously lost in the shuffle and erratically disclosed in his open enclosures.

One of Salamun's early poetic concerns was the relation of objects to their Platonic forms. "In the beginning there was transparency", he wrote in his first collection, evoking that Edenic state in which objects and their names were indissoluble and which Derrida and others after Saussure have worked to debunk. "Things are inscrutable in their craftiness", said Salamun, "unattainable to the rage of the living". The young Salamun explored the frustrated nature of representation and apprehension, applying his mind in 'For Ana' (America, 1973) to the nature of God and meaning, undermining both by developing conceits which enabled him to diverge and dissolve:

No need to sand the stomach walls of Logos from
the inside
out, because it arrived in pieces and was never
really put together.
The parts were set out at intervals like gas pumps
and fields, hence no liquids

trapped in bottles here.
If you take a gallon on the road, you'll use up three
hundred gallons to California, you could even die of
                                  drought
if you had a thousand gallons in your tank. It
                                  vanishes.

Salamun determined that if a theory of Platonic forms only foiled the poet's attempt at perfection, it would have to be replaced by another scheme, at once solipsistic and comprehensive: the self.

Another constricting paradigm to be attacked by the newly-empowered Salamun was his own literary heritage, as in the aptly-titled 'Eclipse':

I grew tired of the image of my tribe
and moved out.

Out of long nails
I weld limbs for my new body.
Out of old rags, my entrails.
A coat of carrion
will be my coal of solitude.
I pluck my eye from the depths of the marsh.
Out of the devoured plates of disgust
I will build my hut.

My world will be a world of sharp edges.
Cruel and eternal.

With that Salamun moved away from his predecessors, whose poetry had sacrificed its spiritual direction to political antagonism and democratic calls-to-arms. He began to mock their agenda, the state and even himself, privileging the personal over the public. His 'Proverbs' are now infamous, ending with an evocation of a figure, like John Gardner's *Grendel*, both fierce and gentle:

1. Tomaz Salamun made the Party blink, tamed it, dismantled it, and reconstituted it.
2. Tomaz Salamun said, Russians Get Out! and they did.
3. Tomaz Salamun sleeps in the forest.

Salamun persisted with this strategy into the mid- and late 1970s, where it assumed an even more impromptu, almost nihilistic aura thanks largely to the style of Ashbery and O'Hara, whom he has credited with opening up in him new avenues of thought and articulation. Salamun rarely lost sight, however, of his native Yugoslavian circumstances;

he said that New York City itself, in fact, was "a lot like the Yugoslav National Army. / A lot of people you never met before". Working from the related premises that "the history of Slavs is, / for example. utterly miserable... / Some small nations biting / each other, because the weather is bad", and that "I'll be a great poet I because they screwed me up", Salamun asserted his vocation vigorously and self-consciously. He spoke of his prayers as song of songs of the Pan-Salamunian religion terribly democratic people's institution which takes in everything yet his negative capability was not really designed to be "democratic": Salamun resisted his precursors' need to speak for their generation, instead mimicking a public voice of consensus in order to demonstrate that his scope was the freedom inherent in the self's multiplicity and possibility. He limited his polemical mode to offering private advice, instructing his daughter Ana, for instance, in the benefits of how "Even so radiates", cautioning her, "Don't believe in yes but, which has cost us thirty percent / of all Slovenian lives".

Rarely has there been a more audacious poet, though at the same time one so unabashed about his own vulnerability. There is something both brash and endearingly insecure about Salamun's early work. In poems such as 'Who's Who', his poem most explicitly indebted to Whitman, Salamun foregrounds braggadocio and a kind of parodied mythic method, but only insofar as that stance veils a more insistent, probably failing attempt at self-conviction:

Tomaz Salamun you are a genius
you are wonderful you are a joy to behold
you are great you are a giant
you are strong and powerful you are phenomenal
you are the greatest of all time...
you are a genius Tomaz Salamun
in harmony with all creation we have to admit that
you are a lion the planets pay homage to you
the sun turns her face to you every day
you are just everything you are Mount Ararat...
you are without beginning or end...
behold the eyes of Tomaz Salamun...
behold his arms behold his loins
behold him striding forth...
you are the *speculum hunanae salvationis*.
beside you every sun appears dark...

The inflated language and the repetition of the line about genius, the obvious allusions to Christ and the Whitmanic corporeality and striding forth, the hyperbole and the mantra-like invocation of his own name: all these serve to reveal, gradually and perhaps against the reader's will, a sense of the speaker's understated charm and essential ego-lessness. We learn nothing about the real Tomaz Salamun from the poem, any more than we do from the conclusion to another poem: "I have a friend whose daughter's name is Breditza. In the evening when they put her to bed she says Salamun and falls asleep". The softness of these lines is not so much a counterpoint to the boldness of 'Who's Who' though; rather, together they begin to unmask the hidden self-deprecation of a poet possessing finely-tuned sensitivities, both on the page and off.

Negative capability allowed Salamun to soak up the world like a sponge and give it back, changed for better or worse, with himself in the rinse. His antiphonal technique was another kind of negativity: emptying the world, rather than apprehending it in toto, in order to find himself in its residual barrenness: "Wildly you cast off what isn't yours", he admitted. He is unashamed of what Stevens or Harold Bloom would call his "capability", yet he expresses gratitude to whomever bestowed it upon him, and his early poems are full of the presence of angels. "Lord I Let me be your supreme law all the way to the end", he asks, adding, "I feel I am being ironed, it doesn't burn at all".

Not all his poems of that time are such serious excursions into being reforged out of his former self, however. In 'September 20, 1972,' for instance, he documents with hilarity and an affected midwest American diction an experience of transformation:

In Iowa City yesterday,
September 20, 1972,1, Tomaz Salamun, underwent
                 a sacramental murder and
resurrection. Oh lordy, hallelujah, I've been born
                 again, I'm soft
and vulnerable. This miracle was all spring in
                 coming.
In America, in England, in Yugoslavia, with love's
mad energy, with horrible pains.

He asked in that same year, "How can we know when it will truly collapse[?]", and perhaps due to the death of Tito in 1980 and the subsequent confusion and frustration in Yugoslavia, Salamun's poetry moves into a noticeably darker phase in his latter work. By this time "sometimes Christ really gets on my nerves", and he ridicules the once tyrannical but now defunct government, saying that because the Communists "didn't liquidate / me at their height, they've missed their chance". His poetry of the 1980s is marked by constant addresses to the reader, making it an erotic discourse of interanimation, as in 'Guilt and Passion' from *The Measure of Time* (1987):

I give just to take back.
To open and penetrate you. To
pierce through the bottom of time, because it is right.

His assertions assume a gravity of tone not to be second-guessed. "The soul is eternal, haven't you heard?" he asks: "It was me who told you that". Salamun begins to distance himself from the overtly slapdash or happy-go-lucky contortions of the previous decade, as his concerns become a reconciliation with historical complicity and the role of the poet in critiquing the ideology and teleology of aesthetics. "We are memory", he says in 'Paris, 1978',

And hence responsible
for the world, although our myth is built into
a machine we no longer control.
Our only real historical chance is
grace, which we alone are helpless to
bestow or set in motion.

His lines become weightier, more elegiac and ponderous. If the earlier poems were bursting with unexpected twists and turns, barrages of freely-associated images and off-the-cuff pronouncements, often spinning pleasurably into oblivion, the later poems require a new discipline: they must be read slowly, with an emphasis placed on a more didactic – though never polemical – resonance. His well-known 'Folk Song' from *Masks* (1980) revises 'History' by universalizing what had once been more specifically personal and funny:

Every true poet is a monster.
He destroys people and their speech.
His singing elevates a technique that wipes out
the earth so we are not eaten by worms.
The drunk sells his coat.
The thief sells his mother.
Only the poet sells his soul to separate it
from the body that he loves.

Some comfort of course has been found in

Slovenia's independence, secured in May 1991 after a brief ten-day war which has already begun to occupy near-mythic status in the Slovenian consciousness. The nation's future is more than ever tied to the West, and American poetry in particular has been increasingly significant there. Salamun's most recent volume, *Ambergris* (1995), much of it translated by Merrill, may be less dark than his work of the 1980s but is no less uncompromising in its vigilance. He has begun to say with confidence again, "The borders of the countries on the earth's crust I hold less than the frostwork on my window", balking at international disputes, or at least ignoring them, and crediting the elemental with recent happiness. Nor has Salamun hardened to the vulnerability that made his earliest work so charming, so that when he writes, "My limbs are Europe's pair of compasses", not only does he speak for Slovenia's entrance into the European community and for his own sense of Alpha-and Omegahood, but we are also reminded of the psychological insecurity of, say, Eliot's admission in *The Waste Land*: "My feet are at Moorgate, and my heart / Under my feet". In one of his earliest poems, Salamun commemorates, "two days ago Eliot died / my teacher", and part of his humility in the later poems is also bound up in acknowledging his poetic roots: the birthday poem for Kocbek is recent, as is a poem containing a smart-aleck passage in which Salamun re-enacts hearing – and possibly reading along with – Ashbery at Cooper Union, 1986:

> And if you did / good that's
> fine, but if you did bad it don't make no
> difference, you're equal / same as the others,
> and the devil don't give a shit who you are or
> whether your name has an umlaut to it".
>
> ('Flow Chart')

So his levity has returned, but not at the expense of tipping his hat where credit is due or of sacrificing his philosophical concerns. He takes great pleasure, in fact, in celebrating his friends in high New York School-style, naming among them his translators Bob Perelman and Anselm Hollo, his ex-wife Maruska Krese, his brother Andraz, his father Branko, as well as Spinoza, Borges, and even Greek gods and goddesses. "Our love makes us perfect friends / down here", reads part of the collection's epigraph from Michelangelo's sonnet for Tomazo de Cavalieri, "but even more, through death, in heaven".

The Four Questions of Melancholy concludes with some of Salamun's most intense, poignant and understated poems to date, largely because he has foregone that annoying habit, so predictable among long-established poets, of evaluating the latitude, longitude and longevity of his work. He entrusts that task to his readers, opting to consider instead, like Czesław Miłosz, the more pressing question of his life's value as it grows older. In his sonnet 'Lacquer,' he senses that "destiny can snuff me out, I feel it now", as he confronts his mortality:

> If destiny doesn't blow on our souls, we freeze
> instantly. I spent days and days afraid
> the sun wouldn't rise. That this was my last day.
> I felt light sliding from my hands, and if I didn't
>
> have enough quarters in my pocket, and Metka's
>   voice
> were not sweet enough and kind and solid and
> real, my soul would escape from my body, as one day
>
> it will. With death you have to be kind.
> Home is where we're from. Everything in a moist
>   dumpling.
> We live only for a flash. Until the lacquer dries.

The dumpling makes Salamun utterly, almost embarrassingly human, and his tribute to his wife (the artist Metka Krasovec, whose painting adorns the cover) is as heartbreaking as modern poetry gets. The poem's counterpart and the collection's concluding sonnet, 'Kiss the Eyes of Peace', speaks of how "life / brings me back to itself". However, it is not given over to a facile celebration born of nostalgia, as Salamun gratefully says that "the cold has done me good". Evoking again that necessary shattering, he leaves us with a stoic but shimmering confession to equal in pathos and tone the terrifyingly beautiful lyrics of Rilke, Glück or Strand:

> In time I might again be able to... Walk
> those roads of dust. Shake the jacket off, if it's
> dusty. There has been too much honey and grace,
>   that's
> all. Too many blessings break a man apart.

Rarely do poets exhibit such an immense range of sensitivities, tones, formal innovation, and understanding of international literary traditions; and Salamun never displays that range for display's sake. There is an intensely philosophical, lyrical and

REVIEWS

wildly humored mind and life behind these poems by a poet who claims to have been "born in a wheat field snapping my fingers". The irony that Salamun enjoys in his poetry is ultimately appropriate in assessing the poetry's value: in his 1971 collection *Pilgrimage for Maruska*, Salamun wrote, "I have six really good poems. I hope I will write more of them". *The Four Questions of Melancholy* confirms that Salamun has produced, during the twenty-five years since, far more really good poems than he had hoped. But he knew that even then, and the joke, of course, is on us.

TOMAZ SALAMUN
THE LETTER

Red, burgundy, blue,
this is my roof, I belong here.
Bread crumbs, jugs, paper and
the wind lifting all of this to the sea.
They bump the hull of a steamboat.
O how I call the body of my younger
self, I would like to hug him.
Why are you not here?
What are you afraid of?
We'll slit the spiral if you want,
we'll crucify the document.
Sun on red bricks in the sunset
will be ours, the continent will be ours.
We'll crush our cradle under the belly of a boat
and get up safe, refreshed.
Come!
Look, I splintered all the New York
bridges into pirouettes,
people are choking, hamsters aren't getting water,
and a huge avalanche,
our sea and a great fair,
kingfishers braking
through the austere air, soft and crystal,
through the father of gelatin,
are landing on our shoulders.

Cabbies are happy.
The world turns up where we rub our sleeves.
We can concentrate the night into a pump and a dumpling.
We dissolve gold.
Something in between wooden tubs and gas cans,
bent blue edge and body made of metal.
We know everything and we know it only here.
Bobby, leave him!

TOM PAULIN
CUAS

A space between rocks; a cavity, a recess; a hollow.

This leather bag – it's a large one –
I don't like the way its flaps
flop wide open
so the whole bag just gapes
has this lolling big gap
that shows the clutter the ramesh inside it
– like two slack tongues
that know they're all wrong
they make a nothing these flaps
a void that looks more than untidy
more than scruffy
I have to buckle down the strap
– the middle one
else the bag's not just throughother
it's a breach in nature
like a sudden slap
in the face
from some unknown creature
and it's rough it's raw
hide that makes me feel iffy
in whatever room where I'm sat
next this dark open maw
that denies – well
the feel of the place
so? you're saying
maybe the thing should be scrapped?
but what interests me
is my own unease
and the way that unease
is close to thinking
to a dull dreamless sleep
state of collapse
or even a last gasp
– it's like a double hasp
two soft saggy hinges
that tend to melt open
and to make me unhappy
– the whole thing's flabby

flabby and scrappy
like a leathery gulch
where I'm slipslittering down a slope
into a much deeper kind of mulch
that might just be
me trying to think
– take water when it's scattered
– round a sink
the word's *japped*
those waterdrops have to be wiped
away like tattered
dirt
like scurf
like matter
because they're junk
brish splatter
– now the same's true
of this leather gab my bag
this sloppy tinker's budget
this Marjorie's wallet
that's no longer raw but
greasy all creashy
so can't be grasped
– it has to be tamed strapped
otherwise it sags
has neither form nor pattern
but like a portable bog
hole – a seanpholl –
makes me feel entrapped

MARK HALLIDAY
HARDENED MUD

On a cold and windy day in March I went out for a walk
all by myself. Significantly this was soon after
the death of a close personal friend or relative. I
went walking beneath the pale chilly sun of March
across a field of hardened mud, moving toward the woods.
(I don't exactly live in the wilderness but
something in my soul is very connected
to the vast elemental power of the wilderness
possibly because as a poet I can relate to forces deeper
than mere human nature.) In my hand I did not have
a take-out coffee cup from Dunkin Donuts because
this just wouldn't fit the mood. The pale sun
rolled (stood? shone? rode?) – the pale sun
among blustery clouds of March rode
indifferently, impervious to the edged winds
whose knives were in turn impervious to it (the sun).
And I walked across that field of humbled weeds
and obscure independent flowers (like poets in a way) thinking
of how we live and die, live only to die, as though
death were the great point of it all somehow, the solution,
the answer to a thousand thorny throbbing questions;
as the woods drew near (or me near them) it was as though
the calm of gray boughs not yet visibly teased by spring
was what I'd meant in the quiet closing lines of many
        previous poems
and I walked slowly, grateful for the wind, the dried puddles,
and my own huge kinds of thoughts; this was
not an experience you have on an average day,
and though I had to turn my collar up
because the wind slashed (clamored, whipped, whickered)
fiercely past my head, and though there was no camera
and no film crew in that entire bleak field
to record my walk, still I was glad
to be alive there, walking, remembering my friend
or relative, and feeling the everything I felt.

M. R. PEACOCKE
CONVERSATION PIECE

Bolt upright on a comfortable chair
an aging patriot of sufficient means
passes the aromatic afternoons
in the address of a lady, coiffed, enhanced, mature.
– Madam, you know how greatly I admire
your passion, your acuity, your clear eye
unwavering like our friendship, your philosophy
(etcetera. Slips to his usual theme, sour
and rebarbative.) Jealousy alone,
not justice, overthrew me . . .
                        – Duty,
my dear sir. One does all that one can.
"Having done all, to stand." A little tea?
The barbarian at the gate. This generation:
barbarity itself, do you not find?
                        – You comfort me,

Madame! My memoirs shall record it:
you are the Cleopatra of your age!
– Flattery, flattery! But time will judge.
That lesser men should denigrate
achievement: that's one's fate; one's lot!
Let history tell. Ignorant partisanship
and jealousy and spite will always carp –
but must not spoil, you know, our *têtes-à-têtes*.
    The afternoon has slipped into its dotage.
Saliva glistens on a mottled lip.
Beyond the window, foliage
nods in a vacant sky. She summons up
a wearying smile. – Courage,
mon cher ami. Come, let me fill your cup.

(Let us forgive one another
our past indiscretions
our inevitable corruptions
our present *petites misères* . . .
I do think Earl Grey is rather
insipid. People overrate –
Where is that car? Make a note
to remind the chauffeur –

Something on television
I had wished to record. The light –)
– Must it be *au revoir?* A little gin?
The evenings now... Yes, it is getting late.
Until we meet again.
Ah – your coat . . .

CHARLES BOYLE
MY OVERTHROW

Bandits from the hills infiltrated the town.
They sold blood-red roses at busy intersections,
whispering through the windows of rush-hour traffic
sublime promises, subversive rumours. They loitered
in stairwells, telling jokes with slow-burning punchlines.
They trained stray dogs to follow me to work
and stand by my office door, whimpering softly.
They handed out fliers for public executions.
They hummed continuous loops of martial music.
They forged my signature and ordered in my name
high-quality luxury goods: an electric wheelchair,
a commemorative dinner service, a shredding machine
into which I fed the instruction manual and three-year
guarantee and – in error, in my eagerness to please –
my life-savings certificates. They played football
on the palace lawn and deliberately kicked the ball
into the path of my car, forcing me to swerve violently
and run over a cat – its eyes softened
in recognition, its entrails were spotted with black.

I got home late. On the mantelpiece,
a single rose, every petal intact. I took off my clothes
and folded them neatly, how I'd folded them for years:
lean years and fat, fallow, madcap, *démodé* years
of unclassifiable material, half eaten by moths,
swaying when I breathed, with the indelible smell of me.

BILLY COLLINS
SILHOUETTE

There is a kind of sweet pointlessness
that can visit at any time,
say this afternoon when I find myself
rustling around in the woods behind the house

and making with my right hand
the head of a duck,
the kind that would cast a silhouetted
profile on a white screen
in a darkened room with a single source of light
if one were in the mood to entertain.

But I am outdoors today and this duck
has a wrist for a neck
and fingers for a beak that never stops flapping,
jabbering about some duck topic,
unless I rotate my arm and let him face me.

Then he stops his quacking
and listens to what I have to say,
even cocking his head like a dog
that listens all day to his master speaking
in English or Turkish or Albanian.

There was talk of war this morning
on the radio, and I imagined the treads of tanks
churning over the young trees again
and planes hacking the air to pieces,
but there is nothing I can do about that
except to continue my walk in the woods
conversing with my hand –

so benign an activity that if everyone
did this perhaps there would *be* no wars,
I might say in a speech
to the ladies' auxiliary of the future farmers of America.

And now it is getting to be evening,
a shift from blue to violet
behind the bare staves of trees.
It is also my birthday,
but there is nothing I can do about that either –
cannot control the hands of time
like this hand in the shape of this duck
who is peers out of my sleeve
with its beak of fingers, its eye of air.

No – I am doing no harm,
but nor am I doing much good.
Would any bridge span a river?
Would a college of nurses have been founded?
Would one stone be placed on top of another
if people let nothing enter their minds
but the non-existent shadows of ducks?

So the sky darkens as always,
and now I am tripping over the fallen branches –
time to head downhill
toward the one burning light in the house
while the duck continues its agitated talk,
in my pocket now,
excited about his fugitive existence,
awed by his sudden and strange life
as each of us should be, one and all.

But never mind that, I think,
as I grab the young trees with my other hand,
braking my way down.
one boot in front of the other,
ready for my birthday dinner,
my birthday sleep, my crazy birthday dreams.

HELEN DUNMORE
THE COFFIN MAKERS

I can't say why so many coffin-makers
have come together here. Company, maybe.
More likely jealousy bites their lips
when they see another's golden coffin
where the corpse will fit like a nut.

No doubt they swap the lids about
at dead of night, scratch the silken cheeks of the wood
so when the mourners come to watch the hammer
bounce off the nails, they'll say it's no good
and in their white clothes they'll swarm
all over the coffin-maker like angry ghosts.

There's no need for it to be like this.
They could lend their tools to one another.
They could watch each other's little shrines
in case the candle goes out. Instead they blow it out
and sourly scour the insides of another cheap
deal coffin for the common man.
How many golden coffins can anyone want?

Of those who appear at the alley-end,
they prefer the advance buyers. It takes know-how
to select a coffin for yourself.
"In our family it's cancer. Allow for shrinkage."
"Dropsy does us. Add it on to the width."
Can a man know the shape of the wood
that will encase him? Can a woman
close her eyes and breathe in the scent of cedar?

These are the ones the coffin-makers like
to sit with by the spirit-lamp. For these they bring out
tea-plums, infuse *Silver Needle*
and drink before they do the measuring.
Time to compare wood-shavings,
rubbing their curls between the fingers. Meanwhile
man and wife from the flat upstairs
take their blue bird for a walk
to the evening park, still in its cage.

FRANCES SACKETT
HOUSE WITH THE MANSARD ROOF

After Edward Hopper

In the stillness of a Sunday morning
You are the only inhabitant
In a world of rising heat.

If you entered any door you would find
Yourself and a dream of yourself
Mingle with the interior dust.

At the railroad, the signal-box windows
Light up with the amber-green of sunset.
Tracks are silver steel
That you can treacherously cross,
But take you nowhere.

In the house with the mansard roof
There is only isolation. Trees cast
Shadows against the white balconies
Like the dark graphics of charcoal,
Awnings billow as a storm rocks the shutters,
Gables and chimney-stacks rise
In a steep confusion and attic windows
Stare up at the moon.

You are a girl in a lonely city
Pushing up a sash window
At the end of another day.
Your bare feet carry shadows
That follow you across the wooden floor.

The storm has brought branches down,
And the trees drip with cool wetness.
You lay your arms on the window frame,
Smoke another cigarette.

ADAM THORPE
GHOSTS
In memoriam. Camargue, 1995

What faces haunt us in our sleep
out of rolling combers
come from the deep; they are our dread

that there's not breath enough to save
the two whom we shall see
strolling over sand towards us, an age from death.

If they are limp in our arms and warm,
what wall now lies between us?
Was it the sea that delivered them so,

or have we blown too softly into their shells?
Let our lungs be taken with theirs
and stretched as trophies on the shelves of Tartarus;

amidst the kite-clattering winds
that they dragged for the elusive, silvery thing
there was air in plenty for our shouts

(as the firm heads rolled in our hands)
of despair. Let the two go well
into their separate sands;

keep about their necks their good-luck chains
and do not clothe their nakedness.
If what slipped on their flesh was our hands

scrabbling for the heart's impatience,
its pluck, pounding our palms upon a drum
that did not sound, then do not blame us

who hold the taste of their death in our mouths,
whose skin is tainted by their failing.
They'll come to Tartarus with the bruises

we planted: how they came by these wounds
is living's business, not to do with there –
that life can be left so easily under a flail of blows

sufficient to strike death cold
and bring the aghast blood back to its senses
makes us wonder why the waters

should ever have delivered us
from the gilled and ghostless world
into this, induced by breath

and the profit of a certain dryness.
Limp amphibians, those who are drowned
are guests among the anchors and the amphorae;

like the other dead, they do not rest for long,
dwelling in our dreams or the gull's mute song.
(Or are in hiding, and have not truly gone.)

LINDA SAUNDERS
BRAQUE'S "COUPLE D'OISEAUX"
from 'Lettera Amorosa'

The conjuror has thrown two souls
into the air. Passing his hands
across the night and opening them
he flung up white wings, lovers,
birds, their bills almost meeting.

Improvised with such precision,
a wonder, their troth as arrows
to the mark, sails of feather –
only the flicker and effort of flight
make these momentary geometries,
only his artistry holds them there
against the deep bell of darkness,
love's pure illusion.

Behind them illegible dusk
written over and over,
lettera amorosa,
as night concentrates desire:
between white profiles of wings,
exactness of beaks, haunting with
birds' eyes, a mask of shadow defines
their shadowless, sweet freedom.

KEITH JEBB
FROM: THE HALFWAY HOUSE

(for the detainees of Campsfield House immigration Detention Centre, past, present and future)

We are bogus –

sometimes we never said what
they say we said

In the corner of the Villa room
a playpen fortress
where the children
practise asylum games

I practise willing
suspension of disbelief

I call it breathing

Wherever we fetch up we
learned unwelcome
here
    we learned breathing
here
    that is merely exchange
of air

Behind grey and white uniforms
a people who don't believe
in themselves choose not
to believe us
      (what
we don't have any right of

listen, it is the concrete flaw
of justice I'm
      already
half-gone, you won't
let us to be with

Why?

are you not running from death?

JUSTO JORGE PADRÓN
THE CHOICE

To Rafael Alberti

With a group of unknown shadows,
I headed for the big warehouse of bodies
For we had orders to be born.
There was such a rush, so many people.
I looked for a head that would be good
For my dreams, and said, "Something romantic,
But with a touch of budding irony
And a pair of believing eyes in which life looms
With its clamour and fire. Can one sign up
For a size larger than one metre eighty?
But if they let me suit my fancy,
I'd ask for some hands, artist's hands,
Delicate, subtle but strong,
To make all they embrace dream.
How delighted I'd be with a mystery voice,
One to gather murmur and flight,
The enigma of autumn hours,
Yes, a sincere voice from a welcoming house
Like a punctual, generous river
In the friendship or love it finds.
I know I've no time left to pick
The great intelligence or will
I'd have wanted, but leave me at least,
Though the last thing, that imagination
Flashing on the ceiling with the light in this room".

Translated from the Spanish by Louis Bourne

SHEENAGH PUGH
CROSS-REALITY

If she can Mary-Sue into his world,
can he to hers? She likes to fancy

how it would happen. The co-ordinates
screw up; land him in Tesco Metro

by the clingfilm.... would he be wearing
that sprayed-on leather suit? Somehow

she's the only one who knows him,
lost in her world, trying not to look it.

She takes his hand; finds him a quiet spot
in the car park; gets a dark-eyed smile

as his outline dissolves into light.
She goes home with his imprint on her eyes.

There'd need to be some fissure, she supposes,
in the fabric of time, some spark

jumping the tracks from one universe
to its parallel . . . would lightning do it?

But her favourite theory is simply
that if she believes in him enough,

belief will call him like a gravitational pull
across realities; harden his edges

– made of words and light as he is –
into flesh she can touch without a doubt.

If electronic signals add up to a picture
on a screen, then why not stories, images

from many minds to a man? What is belief.
but the need for something to be true?

If she waits long enough, he will stand before her,
and she will tell him: *our waiting brought you.*

Note: This poem is taken from a sequence called 'Fanfic', about a woman obsessed with a fictional character. The titles are genres of fan fiction: a Mary-Sue is a fanfic story where a real person crosses into a fictional universe.

GEORGE SZIRTES
DOG-LATIN

The thing that I was was changing. Or was
it wishful thinking? The train rolled on
through a shower, spraying itself in million-
fractured glass and I was lost in the fuzz
of voices – mobile phones, newspapers, leaves
in a long wind. Houses drifted by, caught
in the rain-net, held together by taut
wires: blood, loss, distant relatives
talking in their sleep. Here day and night
made little difference. A man reading the *Mail*
adjusted his glasses. Another had put down
an empty burger-box which opened its bright
yellow mouth and breathed a pungent trail
of garnish across the fast retreating town.

Disjecta membra, little splinters of dog-
Latin from schooldays, as if all life was this,
asserting its privileges, wanting a last kiss
before the terminal parting into fog
and more rain. I looked at the ends of my fingers
parked on the table before me. The train
shook them slightly as it might shake a chain
of events. Everywhere, passengers
were becoming residents, workers, emissaries.
Something was crumbling – a people possibly,
and the flags in the garage had set up
a mad flutter under the bending trees.
It was night or morning or midday, and we
were sitting still, waiting for it to stop.

VERNON SCANNELL
LES BELLES DAMES

Reflected in the troubled looking-glass
of tall shop-windows' tilted, smooth lagoons,
not plain enough for you to make a guess
at colour of the eyes, or even hair –
except that you would know it dark or fair –
they haunt these late autumnal afternoons.

Their other, more substantial, avatars,
released from vitreous immurement, seem
even less attainable than those,
though no less lovely as their dainty feet
chatter like castanets along the street,
while they dance out of sight and into dream.

Their milieu is the City – Rome, New York,
Paris, the Smoke. They are not Zion's daughters,
with wanton eyes and undulating walk,
whose haunches mime the ocean's heaves and dips
and signal to the punters: *Read my hips* –
their message faintest music over waters.

There is, for thwarted seekers, only this
hope of something like a rendezvous,
which has to be in sleep's metropolis
where, white and slender in blue evening air,
as innocent as cigarettes once were,
they open wide their arms; then fade from view.

A SECOND LOOK

Messages from the Edge

PETER BLAND ON THE POETRY OF BRIAN JONES

I VAGUELY REMEMBER a TV documentary about Brian Jones in the late '60's. I think it was in black and white? If not, it should have been. It was the first time I'd seen a real live poet on the box (other than Betjeman pleasantly rabbiting on about churches) and the actuality – almost neutrality – of the poet's modest domestic surroundings, came over with all the power of a mirror image. The poems suggested working-class origins and sympathies, but unlike Dunn's *Terry Street* or, slightly later, Harrison's *School of Eloquence*, this wasn't a two-up two-down sort of world. It was something new... something slightly barren and apart... the poet as post-war domestic man isolated from all the obvious signs of belonging. It was the flip-side of the '60's, with not a Biba or a King's Road in sight. This poet, with his wife... "In sleep I fondle my groin / dreaming your feel"... his kids, mortgage, and blank sheet of paper... "Poets watch / white sheets of paper / for the first signs of words / like rare birdprints / breaking the silence of a snowfield"...was being emotionally and economically exiled from the endless good times that Macmillan and the TV ads promised us. Being young, poor, and having kids, was like being a leper in the early '60's. One moved from juvenile delinquency to middle-age in one stray night. There were no McDonalds or theme parks. The pubs preferred dogs to children. No one would rent you a flat once they saw a pram, and you couldn't afford a car. As a parent, you were sidelined and treated as a second-class citizen. It wasn't long before you hunkered down, fighting back from a crouch.

Published by Alan Ross, Jones's first collection *Poems and a Family Album* (1967) quickly went into three editions. Largely, no doubt, because of the TV programme, but also, I feel, because a new generation recognized where he came from. The territory was the new No-Man's Land of nuclear family isolation and social exclusion. The poems were accessible without being simplistic, and the often touching narratives of man-and-wife isolated in their domestic cul-de-sac were, for all their youthful self-consciousness, skillfully handled... "I know she sleeps. In the room above me / a mind has suddenly ceased to prowl. / And farther off two children sleep / with the primal quick breast-heavings of / stoat or fox. Their sheets are warm as leaves". There was also anger and humour, as in the wonderfully funny (Corso inspired?) 'Stripping Walls', or the equally amusing and incisive 'Chi-Chi': "This is the panda that wouldn't be shagged!". At that time, only Porter perhaps, or Gavin Ewart's *Pleasures of the Flesh*, handled similar material with equal verve.

Two further collections were published by Alan Ross in the late '60's and early '70s: *Interior* (1969) and *For Mad Mary* (1970). They furthered Jones's reputation for well-made narrative poetry that stayed stubbornly close to its primal sources. Despite this early success Jones's poems didn't make many of the '70's and '80's anthologies, but one can imagine that he wouldn't go down well with the largely Oxbridge middle-class go-getters responsible for furthering their own increasingly provincial tastes. As it turned out, Jones's populism was something of a passing fad and he had to dig in rather deeply throughout the Thatcher years. His poems got angrier, often bordering on grumpiness, but he never let go, persistently refusing to discuss his sense of origins or underprivilege in the usual class-conscious sitcom terms... "Remittance defectives, the trepanned crazed, / the obsessives abandoned to their treadmills, / line the seawall, blank as Aunt Sallys. / The Victorian towns crumble their piecrust / derivative splendours and are losing trade". His imagination – with the exception of the odd post-apocalyptic scenario – has always stayed close to his own experiences, to be renamed and made sense of on a day-to-day basis... "For this is the edge, / The final frontier" where "all my years of love and children, / the complex ills of feverish nights, the sweat / and hidden crying simplify to this – a place among the pitiful, a tawdry dream". The looking-in is sometimes more melodramatic than the looking-out, but his best poems from the '70's and early '80's have the edgy clarity of someone who's just clawed his way to the top of the cliff before being startled by the view... "A patina of fuel on half-size margueritas / and a Volvo showroom with a launching party... a Volvo. A sheer and satiny one / stands like a celebrity no one dare approach... It cuts me dead / front on with its blank and armoured face".

What are the poetic values Jones admires most? In his March '68 *London Magazine* review of Elizabeth Bishop's *Selected Poems*, much of what he values in her work might equally apply to what he's striving for in his own. "The syntax is simple. It makes statements, and the statements isolate, focusing our attention on *what is being said*" (italics mine). A sense of immediacy – urgency even – is important. There's no room for frills here, no aesthetic discursions or game-playing with competing realities. We can't imagine him gaily rubbing shoulders with either Ashbery or Olson. "The overriding impression", he says of Bishop's poems, "is of directness and clarity and a fastidious reluctance to commit to imagery". Her poems present a world "of bristling uncanny ordinariness. But then, lacking Bishop's more relaxed stance and her extraordinary eye, how can Jones cut himself down to what he sees as bare essentials without appearing barren, or even boring – for Verdi, that "most unforgiveable of all creative sins". The answer, I would suggest, is in his development of a compellingly fluent poetic voice, together with the previously mentioned sense of immediacy (energy) and a surreal but earthed imagination. Jones's poems are not, as he says of Nemerov, "gracenotes to civilized living". Nor do they like "gesture, mannerism, eclecticism and evasion". Further, as he writes of George Barker's work in a May '68 *London Magazine* review, "I cannot make the effort to enter a world where only words are real". He's increasingly hard on himself, and sometimes on us. We have to glue ourselves to his narratives. When they let us in cleanly that's OK, but they often take the emotional reality prior to the poem, very much for granted. The moral indignation sometimes rushes ahead of his invention and the tone can get a bit preachy. Not often, but enough to sometimes bully his own talent. Nevertheless, poems such as 'On the Edge', 'Cambridge'; 'Class of 19 -', 'Return to Wasteground', and the wonderful 'Overnight...' "Stopping somewhere in England at a place / nondescript"...are icons of the Thatcher years, coming fresh and bitter from the pot, crisply detailed, perfectly focused; and there are a dozen others from those years almost as good.

With his first two Carcanet collections, *The Island Normal* (1980) and *The Children of Separation* (1985) his tone mellows. He writes compellingly about his own domestic failures without self-pity or undue self-regard. From the beginning there have been two distinct approaches, the family "fact" poems, and narrative invention... fictional projections of his inner feelings. The latter help him create a more public scenario, often set in a Tarkovsky-like future, while the persona is usually one of life's extras... a servant of Caesar, a worker in a slaughterhouse, a frontier guard – "You will do what you have always done. Move out". These twin approaches have matured side by side over the years. In the 'Stansted Sonnets', from his last and probably his best collection *Freeborn John* (Carcanet, 1990) he finally bonds with his tribe at a War Memorial... "We have entered the kinship / of Jones: one of the snapped tap-roots / of anonymous names – Betts, Blackman, Bower". He recalls his father's shattered post-war political faith... "Remember Bevan? a haughty blub / of tilted head... The fine contempt of the doomed... You wept / hearing Atlee's curt goodbye". As a fully paid-up member of some beaten-up under-valued pocket of human affection called a family, he embraces his newly-found sense of kinship with "a great sigh of alignment". The dead "squandered by war, tuberculosis, suicide... return in whispered tearful corners". Reconciliation begins to heal the hurt of an England of "winners and losers"... of "vaunting irony" and "curled lip humour" where the "Betts, Blackmans, Bowyers, Browns" have been mainly available "as tombstones". This leveller-like anger at England's waste of human potential arises from a deep love of his inheritance and a real fear for its future. None of which would matter within the context of this essay if he hadn't provided us with some fine poems and a continuous thirty-year commentary from the backrooms of the dispossessed. His voice, at its most focused, is as fluent and imaginative as any over the last quarter of a century. "My passport said *British*. / I resented that. / The boots slamming on continents. / The cuffs stiff with insensitivity/ at the end of jungles. / I wanted to write *English* / for its sly evasive music / and sensual valleys, / its twists and turns and unlocatable / laconic heart".

We're badly in need of a Jones *Selected*. All his past work is currently out of print, except for *Freeborn John*, of which there are less than thirty copies left. No new book has appeared for almost a decade. I doubt that the fires are out, but the best of what we already have will almost certainly outlast the decades with which it was so intimately and courageously concerned.

The Wrong End of the Rainbow

STEPHEN BURT ON RANDALL JARRELL

I'VE FELT SURE for several years now that the American poet Randall Jarrell (1914-1965) wrote some of the best poems of the century – that he ought to be read wherever his most talented contemporaries – Larkin, MacNeice, Bishop, Berryman, Robert Lowell – are read. Jarrell's work can look at first (and sometimes at last) less technically consistent, less made, than theirs. Like his masters – Wordsworth, Browning, Rilke, Hardy – Jarrell can be hard to praise in technical terms: he wrote some one-page, well-made, well-closed, image-based poems, but his real powers often lay in forms longer or shorter. Almost everything he accomplished can prompt accusations of sentimentality, of flatfootedness – accusations which in turn generate defences like this one. I've tried to explain Jarrell's craft in some longer essays (one's out this year in *Metre*): here I want to show you two kinds of poems at which he excelled, and to raise him above two categories into which he's sometimes shunted.

One category: War Poets. Jarrell was the Best American Poet of World War II: his work training pilots helped him write 'The Death of the Ball Turret Gunner', a poem you've probably seen if you know Jarrell's name:

From my mother's sleep I fell into the State
And I hunched in its belly till my wet fur froze.

Six miles from earth, loosed from its dream of life,
I woke to black flak and the nightmare fighters.
When I died they washed me out of the turret with a
    hose.

The poem is, you'll agree, a memorably startling, heterogeneous yoking-together of birth-trauma and violent death, womb and turret: that's why it wound up in so many anthologies that Jarrell dreaded its floods of reprint requests, lest the future think him "a poet of one poem". And who would expect the author of such a horrifyingly Freudian sketch to have written short love poems as good, and as tender, as 'The Meteorite'?

Star, that looked so long among the stones
And picked from them, half iron and half dirt,
One; and bent and put it to her lips
And breathed upon it till at last it burned
Uncertainly, among the stars its sisters –
Breathe on me still, star, sister.

Like most of Jarrell's best poems, this one depends on the fiction it builds of a listener – her attentions, at first as unlikely and distant as starlight, and then as close as the breath in a kiss, cue the whole speech-act. (Jarrell's widow Mary, who has just published a memoir, *Remembering Randall* (HarperCollins), says it was the first poem he wrote for her.)

The unmistakable emotion depends for its pace and affective power on some unobvious technique. The poet-lover-stone called "One" rests solitary in the middle of the poem, after the five lines' sole enjambment, as if grounded there – until the female star elevates and embraces it. The poem begins as a declarative sentence, and readers might expect it to end as one: "Star, that looked so long... and bent... and breathed... you will / will not look / bend / breathe". Instead Jarrell switches to the imperative and introduces a first-person pronoun: the change brings the "star" closer to the poet, makes the first few lines seem by comparison with the last a too-remote, and at last removed, mask for the beloved.

Stars in love poems normally keep their distance (compare Keats' 'Bright Star', Auden's 'The More Loving One'); this star turns out unexpectedly present, close enough to heed a request.

Another category: Poet-Critic. Jarrell was the most controversial, funniest, and (by today's tastes) most nearly prescient critic of his time, extolling early Auden, Whitman, Frost, Bishop, and, later, the fiction of Chekhov, Kipling, Christina Stead. Of Stead's *The Man Who Loved Children*, Jarrell remarked,

> The book has an almost frightening power of remembrance; and so much of our earlier life is repressed, forgotten, both in the books we read and the memories we have, that this seems friendly of the book, even when what it reminds us of is terrible.

Jarrell's poems reveal their own "frightening powers of remembrance", seeing lives as doomed or joyful wholes – looking back to childhood, forward to age. The poems that do so most fully are longish, sad, stream-of-consciousness semi-narratives – of Jarrell's childhood year in Hollywood ('The Lost World'), of a troubled young New York father ('Hope'), of a bright fourteen-year-old girl in the Thirties ('The Night Before the Night Before Christmas'), of an aging, never-married, painter ('The End of the Rainbow'). Among these poems, 'The Lost World' remains the most widely-appreciated; 'The Night Before...' now seems the most interesting in terms of literary history, society, politics. And the neglected 'The End of the Rainbow' may be the most concentratedly powerful: its retiring artist, alone with her dog Su-Su (her fourth by that name), acts out the hypothesis Jarrell spelled out in another poem, 'A Girl in a Library': "The ways we miss our lives are life".

It was Yeats who wrote that his whole life seemed to him a preparation for something he never accomplished; it was Jarrell who made a style to fit that feeling – in 'The End of the Rainbow' the sentences seem never to end, because they and their thoughtful, pathetic speaker (named Content, as other women are named Prudence or Chastity) seek ends, goals, contents, she can never find. Alone "here at the wrong end of the rainbow", Jarrell's artist sees her California beach blur into a fairy-tale underworld, her life merge with her fairy-tale art, and both with her stock of mixed-up proverbs:

> Voices float up: seals are barking
> On the seal-rocks as, once, frogs were croaking
> On rushy islands in the marsh of night.
>
> Voices – the voices of others and her voice
> Tuned flat like a country fiddle, like a Death
> Rubbing his bow with resin at a square-dance –
> Voices begin: ... *A spider a frying pan, and tonic-pop*
> *And – fancy! – put tomatoes in their chowder.*
> *Go slow. Go slow. You owe it to yourself.*
> *Watch out for the engine. You owe it to yourself.*
> *Neither a borrower nor a lender be.*
> *Better to be safe than sorry.*
> *Better to be safe than sorry. Say to yourself,*
> *Is it my money they're asking for, or me?*

Nothing Content does or makes seems to her more durable than these half-remembered recipes, these all-too-practical clichés: she has sought ends and found, uselessly, means. In Content's marsh

"The voices tune themselves / And keep on tuning: there is no piece, just tuning". Neither life nor art, real seals nor frog-princes, can give Content the sense of worth she wants for her life, or (failing that) for her art –

> The gift for life, the gift of life
> Are rarer, surely, than the gift of making
> In a life-class, a study from the life
> Of some girl, naked for an hour, by the hour;
> Of making, from an egg, a jug,
> An eggplant, at cross purposes on drapery,
> A still-life; of rendering, with a stump,
> Art-gum, and four hardnesses of charcoal, life
> Whispering to the naked girl, the naked egg, the naked
> Painter: "What am I offered for this frog?"

Content keeps living, just as words like "life" keep repeating in Jarrell's lines, even as they lose their apparent value. Her discontent leads into, and resembles, Jarrell's vexation over the worth of art, the place of poems, as putative ends in themselves, in a society that treats them (and what society has not?) mostly as means, as media, as vehicles – to prestige, social change, money. However we manage to measure ourselves, others – the poem remembers – measure our worth by the money-value of work we do, until we feel that it can be only a means to a means, and ourselves only means to it: that, as the child in in 'The Lost World' decides, "the fact of life, / The secret the grownups share, is what to do / To make money". And even if we are lucky enough to make good poems, good paintings, works others will consider as ends (though how could we, their makers, ever know?) – even then, we are not immune, as Jarrell knew, from anomie, from endlessness. Hearing the voices of endless tuning, endless living, Content asks:

> "Look at my life. Should I go on with it?
> It seems to you I have... a real gift?
> I shouldn't like to keep on if I only...
> It seems to you my life is a success?"

Death answers, *Yes. Well, yes.* [...]

> The local colors fade:
> She hangs here on the verge of seeing
> In black and white,
> And turns with an accustomed gesture
> To the easel, saying:
> "Without my paintings, I would be –
>   why, whatever would I be?"

'The End of the Rainbow' may be hard to excerpt, because part of its strength lies in its continuousness, as Content's associations and memories play out over eleven broad pages of Jarrell's *Complete Poems*. I have chosen to sample it for you because (as far as I know) nobody loves it as much as I love it (yet); if you like it even a little, check out his more shapely triumphs: anthology-pieces like 'The Woman at the Washington Zoo', 'Next Day', 'A Girl in a Library', 'Eighth Air Force', 'Jerome,' 'Moving,' 'A Front,' 'The Lonely Man,' or 'Second Air Force' or the perfectly heartbreaking semi-dramatic monologue 'The Player Piano'. If part of Jarrell's gift involved his empathy – with the painter Content, with the Ball Turret Gunner – another part was bound up with his sense of futility, of how little poems can do to redeem a whole life. How do we respond to this sense, to the knowledge that for all but a very few of us, almost nothing we do or discover or feel will survive us for long? Mostly, we don't; sometimes, we become kinder; when lucky, we fall, and stay, in love; occasionally we make art as good as Jarrell's. There is no good reason for us to keep missing it.

STEPHEN BURT
THE WIND FROM THE 1950s

> Randall Jarrell's daughters are still riding
> Behind him in an open-topped sports car
>
> Of 1957, streamlined, plush
> And spotlessly maintained. They look back from it

With hair too short to be blown back by the wind,
They look back as if clinging to the spine

And haunch of the leopard that sprints in the National Zoo,
Whose enlightened hosts have built for it

A cage like a savannah in a cage.
They're really his stepdaughters. From the nest

The driver's seat makes for him, from his split-
At-both-ends beard and tipped-back shades, he grins,
His rose cheeks taut. He looks at home among them.

* * *

Election Night: Rock Creek sorts coloured stones,
Turns mill wheels, joins a never-used canal

(Steam trains took all its traffic from day one).
Counting close races on the radio,

I thought of justice, one of the mud-choked paths,
Developing, returning to no source;
Of silver crowns coins thrown in water raise;

Of Katharine Hepburn on the roof in *Desk Set*,
Skyscraper-top wind cooling her bag lunch.

She's a reference librarian scared of losing her job
To the megacomputer whose hierophant and guide

Is Spencer Tracy, who can't tie his shoes.
He staggers with the luggage of the breeze

Beating about his coat, dragging him down,
Then lifts his sandwich from his lips and asks

(Reads from his clipboard) *When you meet someone
For the first time, what's the first thing you notice?*

His checklist's flapping: *Eyes. Hair. Accent. Gait.*
Reaction shot. Amused. *Red hair, green eyes:
Whether that person is (pauses) a man, or a woman.*

Cooking with Relish

by Lawrence Sail

GÜNTER GRASS
Selected Poems 1956–1993
translated by Michael Hamburger
Faber, £9.99
ISBN 0571 19518 0

THIRTY YEARS ON, it is good to have a successor to the Penguin *Poems of Günter Grass* – and a bilingual edition, too. Covering the period from Grass's first published poems, but excluding the 1997 volume *Fundsachen für Nichtleser* (*Found Things for Non-Readers*), this new selection draws most fully on the 1960 collection *Gleisdreieck* (*Triangular Junction*) which accounts for 25 of the 51 poems here. In his preface the translator, Michael Hamburger (who also translated all but eight of the Penguin selection) writes that "it has been Günter Grass's distinction to strike a peculiar balance between the usually irreconcilable extremes of personal, almost obsessive idiosyncracy... and of social conscience and social vision...". Certainly there is plentiful evidence of the poet's range, from the pungent epigrams of the earlier poems to surreal conceits, fables with a social or political dimension and a few rather more personal poems. Sometimes the poems carry reminders of the novels, for instance 'Family Matters', where the museum in which "our aborted children, pale, serious embryos, / sit there in plain glass jars" recalls the office of Dr. Hollatz, in *The Tin Drum*, where the five year old Oskar's screams shatter the doctor's collection of bottled embryos.

Grass achieves some of his best effects by the kind of incongruity suggested in 'Comforted', where men are seen as big, unweaned babies, or in the sinister implications of 'Nursery Rhyme', apparently Grass's own favourite among his poems (though in the Penguin selection present only in the Introduction, in German, where Hamburger quotes it as an instance of an untranslatable poem). He is deft at heightening the atmosphere of his poems by a number of recurrent motifs, many of them suggesting secrecy, authority, control and, with that, the possibility of exclusion: wardrobes, keys, admission tickets, erasers. Recurrence plays an important structural part, too, in such poems as 'The Great Rubblewoman Speaks', where much of the impetus and verve are achieved by the urgent reiterations at the beginning of each of its 23 verses ("Where where where where / have the old gallants gone.. ?"; "She she she she / digs away the sand under the pillar"); or as in 'Sudden Fright', a single sentence energetically propelled by "when" at the beginning of each verse, with the one main verb kept for the end of the poem. Similarly, four of the five verses of 'The Scarecrows' begin with "I don't know". Other poems rely on bizarre images and associations: among the most memorable are 'Magical Exercise with the Brides of Christ' with its flying nuns, and 'Chefs and Spoons' where a quirky logic finally takes over:

> Then stay, spoon, go.
> To whom spoon, spoon leads where.
> What time spoon, spoon was late.
> Who stirs me, stirs me where.
> Over and over cuts whose hair.
> Then stay, spoon, go – and do not tell me where.

Quite other, and conspicuous by their infrequency, are poems such as 'Marriage', 'Hymn' and 'Love Tested' in which, while never letting go of wit or becoming sentimental, Grass allows himself a degree of tenderness. In this mode 'Leavetaking', a dream of all creation extinguished that nonetheless ends with "one rat that gave birth to nine / and was blessed with a future", stands out. The longest poem in the book, 'Do Something', is very different again, as is the one that precedes it, 'Powerless, with a Guitar'. Both tackle head-on the powerless of the individual confronted with power and violence: though they must have been written in the fifties, it is the sixties which they call to mind. Grass has no illusions: protest is impotent, and the challenge of the human imperative to do something shrinks to a mocking or despairing refrain. The events of 1999 give his poem a new topicality, and poetry itself does not escape:

> Just as steel has its booms, so poetry has its booms.
> Rearmament opens markets for anti-war poems.
> The cost of production is low.
> Take an eighth of righteous indignation,
> two eighths of everyday annoyance
> and five eighths – to heighten that flavour –

of impotent rage.
For medium-sized feelings against the war
are cheaply obtained
and have been shopsoiled ever since Troy.

Inevitably, the poem leads only to the dead end of impotent rage: but Grass wittily sidesteps and offers instead a cooking lesson in the poem which follows, 'The Jellied Pig's Head'. This *tour de force* substitutes for powerlessness's recipe for despair one whose main ingredients are compelling vividness and an attention to anatomical detail which could induce revulsion as much as salivation.

The most recent work here is *Novemberland*, the sequence of thirteen sonnets with which the book ends. According to Hamburger this is "at once the most topical of his later sequences and the most indebted to baroque prosody and conceits". The topicality takes the form of a wintry view in keeping with the title, a disenchanted vision of a Germany beset by fear and a self-hatred expressed as hatred of others, the mentality of "fortress Novemberland". Here no recipe can quite assimilate the tough ingredients of money, power, anger and politics. But whatever Grass's debt to "baroque prosody and conceits" and whatever his intention, in translation the sequence too often just reads clumsily, with vocabulary and sentence structure distorted, sometimes for the sake of rhyme. For instance, the closing lines of 'Gale Warning' ("Schon wieder, angekündigt, ein Orkan zuviel, / der keine Grenzen kennt, klopft an und fordert laut Asyl") become: "And, forecast, yet another most unwelcome such / gate-crashes every frontier, loud-mouthed. It's too much". Or 'Before the First Sunday in Advent', where the translation of "*Hagebutten glühn*" as "rosehips cast their sheen" seems too exotic for the context of a "stripped garden", too obviously there to provide a rhyme with "gasoline" at the end of the line before.

Whether, as the blurb claims, this selection "encapsulates one of the defining poetic *oeuvres* of our time", is open to doubt. But it does offer a further and enjoyable insight into the mind of a writer who, as his novels amply demonstrate, always cooks with relish.

GEORG TRAKL
GRODEK

In the evening the autumnal forests resound
With deadly weapons, the golden plains
And blue lakes, above them the sun
Rolls more darkly by; night enfolds
The dying warriors, the wild lament
Of their broken mouths.
But in the grassy vale the spilled blood,
Red clouds in which an angry god lives,
Gathers quietly, lunar coldness;
All streets lead to black decay.
Beneath the golden boughs of night and stars
The sister's shadow reels through the silent grove
To greet the ghosts of heroes, their bleeding heads;
And the dark flutes of autumn sound quietly in the reeds.
Oh prouder sorrow! you brass altars
Today an immense anguish feeds the mind's hot flame,
The unborn descendants.

Translated from the German by Margitt Lehbert

TWO POEMS BY ROBERT SAXTON
TO ORPHEUS, II, XV
after Rilke

You are the unsurprised open mouth in the water-garden,
Repeating the one pure phrase of your one true fable,
All those skeins of water bundled into the one cable,
Spooling out of your marble mask – my gift, my pardon.

Miles off, aqueducts tilt themselves to their commission
Infinitesimally. Towards you down the Apennine slopes
Past graves of forgotten loves they bring their deposition.
Syllables abseil from your bearded chin on liquid ropes

Into the basin below. Lichen-crusted, chthonic, Greek,
This is the intimate marble ear into which you speak,
Lug of the half-sleeping earth mother, always intent

Upon her own monologue. I slip a jug under the stream.
She bridles at my saucy interruption to her theme
And, in the change of pitch, voices, mildly, her dissent.

TO ORPHEUS, I, I
after Rilke

A tree grew, like an embryo, as Orpheus cleared his throat
To sing. Its roots coiled through the uninhabitable maze
Of the ear. Leaves uncurled from branches, note by note –
A fresh life, beckoning. Slowly, through the morning haze,

Animals ventured from their ancient forest runs, shunning
The thicket's subterfuge – till every nest, earth, den, lair
Was deserted. If they came so quietly, in that seed-flecked air,
It wasn't that they were shy, or brutishly dumb, or cunning,

It was just that they wanted to listen. Roar, shriek and cry
Subsided in their hearts. And whereas before they couldn't lay
Claim to so much as a rough hut to offer or receive prayers,

Only a wind-thrashed shelter nailed up out of their scares
And cravings, with shuddering birches for an entranceway,
You sang them a temple – a gilded roof beneath a leaden sky.

ZBIGNIEW HERBERT
BREVIARY

Lord
>   I know that my days are numbered
>   there are only a few left
>   Barely enough in which to gather the sand
>   my face will be covered with
>
>   I won't now be able
>   to do justice to those who've been wronged
>   nor yet to ask the forgiveness
>   of all those I have hurt
>   because of this my soul is heavy
>
>   my life
>   should have been a circle
>   it should have ended like a well-composed sonata
>   but now I can see exactly
>   in the moment before the coda
>   broken chords
>   misapplied colours and words
>   dissonance clatter
>   tongues of chaos
>
>   why couldn't
>   my life
>   have been like ripples over a pond
>   rising from infinite depths
>   a beginning which grows
>   orders itself in grain degree
>   fold so as to die quietly
>   at your inscrutable knees

Translated from the Polish by Clive Wilmer and George Gömöri

PIOTR SOMMER
HI HELENA

Helena asks, how's Jola's thesis.
So far no more than ten pages.
Helena nods. I guess she thinks
about the burnt-out, overdrawn
potential of some young women
she knows who might still have a child.
Does she have enough time for it?
Well yes, I say, as if my belly hurts.
Helena agrees that it's all about just getting going.

You can't get away from numbers. Not quite
ten pages of a belated master's thesis,
not quite six hours sleep, a child
or two. In a few years
a next-of-kin dies and the young thirty-somethings
will open up the deadly flat
to live in it, like it or not
they'll move in, like it or not they'll forget
who left it to them.
Death wishes you all the very best.

But then what's the hurry, Helena adds.
Her husband got fired last year.
It's possible, even certain
that everything boils down to personally
certifying a few of the things that count. Many
won't even know
the story. I'm raising all this
on the last day of August, a transparent night,
while well-wishing death keeps working
on another world, for as and those we like.

Translated from the Polish by Halina Janod and M. Kasper (we apologise for mis-spelling his name in Vol 88 No 4, p.38; furthermore the poem by Zbigniew Machej (p.41) was co-translated by Piotr Sommer and M. Kasper).

Wise Acre

By Vernon Scannell

JAY PARINI

Robert Frost: A Life

Heinemann £20.00
ISBN 0 434 00166 X

"A SHILLING LIFE will give you all the facts", famously wrote W. H. Auden in the 1930s, which perhaps tells us more about monetary inflation than the biographer's art, but a good biography must do more than simply relate the principal events of its subject's life, especially if, as in the case of Jay Parini's *Robert Frost*, the subject is an eminent poet and a more than usually complex character. The nature and value of the work must be examined and assessed and related to the character of the poet and the changing circumstances of his life. The facts of Frost's life are fairly well-known, as well over a dozen biographies and memoirs have been published since his death in 1963, including the massive three volume job by Lawrance Thompson, completed by Thompson's student, R. H. Winnick, in 1976.

Thompson' *Life of Frost* is notoriously critical of the poet's moral character and conduct, his egoism, bigotry, chauvinism and frequent harsh treatment of his family. Parini, while acknowledging his indebtedness to Thompson's work, has clearly set out to do a corrective whitewash. While he can't deny that Frost was, both in his youth and increasingly in maturity and old age, racist, homophobic and politically reactionary – he detested Franklin D. Roosevelt and was contemptuously opposed to the New Deal programme of social and economic reform – Parini tries, unconvincingly, to explain, if not justify, these attitudes by saying of him, "He is not a conservative in the contemporary sense. He is an agrarian free-thinker, a democrat with a small 'd'".

That Frost could be mean, vindictive and vain is undeniable but he was capable of real generosity. He was the principal facilitator in gaining Ezra Pound's release from St Elizabeth's Hospital in 1958 despite the fact that he was bitterly hostile to the arch-modernist who, he said, encouraged his followers "to seek originality by subtracting meter and meaning from their work".

The relationship between the life and work of any artist has always been a matter for interesting speculation but finally what really counts is the quality of the artefact that he creates. In recent times the biography and letters of Philip Larkin have provoked a lot of conjecture about the man's political and moral attitudes and have prompted, among some radical and feminist readers, negative revisions of judgement on the quality of the poetry. But the best of his poems are without significant political content and sensible readers of whatever ideological persuasion should be able to enjoy them.

The same is true of Frost. The details of his life are both fascinating and disturbing. His early years were spent in San Francisco until, at the age of eleven, on the death of his drunken and irresponsible newsman father, he moved with his mother to Massachusetts where at the Lawrence High School, he met Elinor Miriam White whom he was to marry in December 1895 at the age of twenty-one. He spent a couple of years at Harvard from 1897 to 1899, then in October 1900 he settled down with Elinor, who had by then borne him two children, on a farm in New Hampshire bought for him by his grandfather.

As a farmer he was less than successful: his habit of staying up into the early hours reading and writing poetry and his inability to get out of bed in the morning were not the only reasons for his poor performance and in 1906 he took a job teaching at Pinkerton Academy, a New Hampshire secondary school.

In 1912 he sold the farm and, with his wife and family (there were now four children) he sailed for England, where he met and formed a brief but profound friendship with Edward Thomas and published his first volume of poetry, *A Boy's Will*, followed a year later by *North of Boston*.

In 1915 he returned to America and to farming but by then his poetic reputation was well on its way to becoming firmly established and he was soon spending far more time teaching in various colleges and in giving poetry readings than working on the land.

A third volume, *Mountain Interval*, was published in 1916 to great and well-deserved acclaim (it contained such gems as 'The Road Not Taken', 'Birches' and 'The Hill Wife' which were to become widely anthologised and greatly loved by countless readers on both sides of the Atlantic) and he continued to develop the persona of shrewd, witty and pragmatic rural wiseacre that charmed his admirers.

From then on his reputation grew rapidly and honours were lavishly bestowed on him. In 1924 his fourth book, *New Hampshire*, won him the first of four Pulitzer Prizes and the awards of honorary doctorates began to proliferate on an almost embarrassing scale.

His domestic and emotional life, however, was by no means tranquil. Frost and Elinor had already lost two children in infancy and in 1934 their daughter Marjorie, died of tuberculosis. Earlier, in 1920, his sister Jeanie had been confined to a State asylum where nine years later she died at the age of fifty-three. After her confinement, Parini tells us, "...he rarely saw her again, finding visits too painful to withstand".

The death of Elinor in 1938 and the suicide of the Frosts' son, Carol, two years later are reported but the reader learns little of Frost's reactions to these traumatic events. When, soon after his wife's death, the poet begins an affair with Kay Morrison, the wife of a college professor and over twenty years younger than Frost, Parini is tactful to the point of euphemism, referring to her as *amanuensis* to the aged poet. On the whole, though, the life is well told and the last trip the old man makes to England to receive his Oxford doctorate and the visit to Edward Thomas's old home movingly described.

The attempts to relate the work to the life, however, are a lot less satisfactory. Confidence in Parini as a literary critic is shaken a little in the purely narrative sequences by the fairly frequent misuse of ordinary words. Early in the book he refers to Frost's father as "brashly" resigning his job where he must surely mean "rashly". I thought this might be carelessness or a misprint until, a few pages later, he writes that Frost "...absorbed (sic) from his father a great deal including a feral (sic) drive to make something of himself" and he uses "narcissism" where he means "egotism". Misreadings of whole poems, however, are a much more serious matter.

Parini is subject to that common perversion among many of the older American academics of reading sexual significance into texts which, to the ordinary poetry-reader, would be quite free from such an interpretation. Of the fine early poem, 'Mowing', he writes: "...this is a poem about writing, a poem about the process of knowing, a poem about the sexual act and what it means". You could have fooled me and, I suspect, umpteen thousands of other readers who know the poem well as a beautifully written account of performing a specific task and the satisfaction derived from it and, by implication, other tasks, though hardly the "task" of procreation.

'Birches', Parini informs us, "...is, as much as anything, a poem about onanistic fantasy" and he triumphantly quotes:

> One by one he subdued
>   his father's trees
> By riding them down
>   over and over
> Until he took the stiff
>   ness out of them,
> and not one but hung
>   limp....

Geddit? Stiffness? Hung limp? Must be on about willies. Just as obtuse – Parini's tendency to see wholly coincidental echoings of isolated words from other poets' work as evidence of "influence" or deliberate quotation. For instance he gives us the lovely late lyric, 'Questioning Faces' and says, "The poem seems to beckon, obliquely, to Wallace Stevens, who ended 'Sunday Morning' with a brilliant image of pigeons 'sinking downward to darkness, on extended wings'". That takes a bit of beating for sheer silliness.

For anyone unfamiliar with the broad details of Frost's life, Parini provides a readable, though sanitized, account, but for an illuminating examination of the work the reader must look elsewhere or, best of all, go to the poems.

THE CLASSIC POEM

SELECTED BY JAMES KEERY

THE TITLE POEM of Singer's only collection, which appeared in 1957, 'Still and All' is addressed to the poet's readers and precursors, in particular to W. S. Graham and Dylan Thomas ("After the first death ..."). It is a distillation of their "ways / Of speech", but also of ours, for there is nothing exclusive about the reciprocity by which language is "Given" and "Returned". The bell and the sundial suggest a churchyard, the speaker perhaps a dead poet, whose "quiet / Survival's answer" is made from the grave but also from Hopkins's "higher cleave" of posthumous being.

Singer can be as down-to-earth and as up-to-date as Larkin or Amis – "A fig for poets is his anthem as / He dons his shirt washed out in brilliant Daz'" – but, in his eyes, immortality is no stale cliché but rather "the least preposterous / Of the infinities that robe you round". His attitude to the new Movement was one of contempt. He expressed it frequently, in pubs, at parties and in print, and, throughout the 1950s, he can be observed gaining and losing a reputation at the same time. Apocalyptic poetry is still in eclipse, and certainly, in Singer's own sharp phrase, "eternity's extreme unction" can be hard to take. But nothing could be less unctuous than his amazing poetry, a fusion of Apocalyptic sublimity with the principled intelligence of the Movement.

BURNS SINGER
STILL AND ALL

I give my word on it. There is no way
Other than this. There is no other way
Of speaking. I am my name. I find my place
Empty without a word, and my word is
Given again. It is nothing less than all
Given away again, and all still truly
Returned on a belief. Believe me now.
There is no other. There is no other way.

These words run vertical in their slim green tunnels
Without any turning away. They turn into
The first flower and speak from a silent bell.
But underneath it is as always still
Truly awakening, slowly and slowly turning
About a shadow scribbled down by sunlight
And turning about my name. I am in my
Survival's hands. I am my shadow's theme.

My shadow's ground feeds me with roots, and rhymes
My statement over. Its radius feeds my flames
Into a cool tunnel. And I who find your ways
About me (In every part I find your ways
Of speech) pierce ground and shadow still. The light

THE CLASSIC POEM

Is struck. Its definition makes me my quiet
Survival's answer. All still and all so truly
Wakening underneath me and turning slowly.

It's all so truly still. I'll take you into
The first statement. I'll take you along cool tunnels
That channelled light and petalled an iridescent
Symmetry over my bruised shadow. And yes
I'll take you, and your word will follow me,
Till definitions gather distilled honey
And make their mark the fingerprints of light.
I am, believe me then, the name I write.

I lie here still. Yes, truly still. And all
My deliberate identities have fallen
Away with the word given. I find my place
In every place, in every part of speech,
And lie there still. I let my statements go.
A cool green tunnel has stepped in the light of my shadow.
There is no way round it. It leads to the flower
Bell – that swings slowly and slowly over.

An extended edition of *Collected Poems* by Burns Singer (1928-1964) is due from Carcanet in the autumn.

IN APPRECIATION OF

Bill Turner (1927–1998)

by Gael Turnbull

WILLIAM PRICE TURNER published under the name "W. Price Turner" until about 1979, when he began to use "Bill Turner", the label under which he had published the last five of the six novels ("thrillers") which gave him some precarious income for a few years.

Most of his personal life, including periods as Gregory Fellow at Leeds and writer-in-residence at Glasgow, is not relevant to this appreciation but some understanding of his early years is helpful. Although born in York, his parents returned to their native Scotland when he was still an infant. Forced to leave formal education when only 14, he grew up, and spent his early adult years, in Glasgow, and throughout his life, in his words, was "permanently encumbered by a Scottish accent".

From 1951 to 1957, still in Glasgow, he edited and hand printed 15 issues of *The Poet*, a truly "little magazine", and was justly proud of its quality and international scope, and that it featured early poems by "names" later to become well known. [see account in *Poetry Matters* (Peterloo, autumn 1984).]

APPRECIATION

Throughout his life he published regularly in magazines, wrote occasional reviews and other items, and had plays and poems broadcast. In later years he found amusement, as well as income, winning poetry and verse competitions (entered anonymously). Mostly rebuffed by major publishers, his books and pamphlets in fact sold well. The only one still in print is *Fables for Love, New and Selected Poems* (Peterloo, 1985).

His first full collection was *The Rudiment of an Eye* (1955) where the most achieved poem is probably 'Idealist', but the opening lines from 'Egotist' give a more immediate impression of some major characteristics: the use of imagery, the compression and sharpness of phrasing, and an element of mockery amid celebration.

> I have a rage trained
> on many an old hurt,
> but I do not feed it;
> I keep it chained
> in a sly cellar
> where it snarls at its own smell.

The Flying Corset (1962) is notable for more overtly satirical pieces (the three "Kilroy" villanelles being particularly accomplished) flashing with what one reviewer remarked as "progressive energy".

The title poem starts:

> At last, the flying corset, the first
> manufactured garment to give genuine uplift,
> tested and certified, as real as thirst,
> and as exhilarating to indulge...

The device is sustained for 77 lines, making a virtuoso elaboration of the central metaphor, and using it as a commentary on the human situation, mixing derision with wry understanding: should we laugh or despair?

Another good example of his use of metaphor (and ironic fantasy) is the title poem of *The Moral Rocking-Horse* (1970) which begins:

> Wanted: Good Home for Moral Rocking-Horse.
> I just fell off again. It's clear
> my riding days are strictly limited,
> but that unbreakable brute
> needs exercise I can't maintain.

The poem ends with the comment of a bystander;

> in honest puzzlement:
> *But it gets you nowhere.*
> And that's perfectly true.
> I wonder where he wanted to go.

Of the newer poems in *Fables for Love* the most striking, for invention and elaboration, are 'Cuckoo Clock and Camera: A Dialogue', and 'A Prune Named Wittgenstein' which imagines the master reincarnated as a prune speaking to his disciple Rodney:

> If you knew how I long to be assimilated! Yet I fear that your logical tapeworm may urge you to deny me. Rodney, I could explain everything, but it would take too long. Consider how Leibnitz and Newton's protracted debate sent God to sleep...

and goes on to range across the problems and paradoxes of thought and human frailty, ending with:

> ... has not your meekest student
> advised you where you can shove
> Wittgenstein?

Not included in this volume is his 'Mexican Jumping Bean' which he categorised as "a longish poem". The "Bean" is, of course, not a bean but a chrysalis and becomes both the subject and characterisation of a poem which he sustains and varies for 264 compact lines that twitch with impudent energy.

Not all his work is so emblematic. There are many lyrical pieces (his Glasgow poems and 'The Back Court Piper' sequence) but also direct and personal poems charged with intense feeling, particularly 'Visitation', 'Progress Report', 'Reproaches', 'As Advertised' and 'Idealist'. These do not easily lend themselves to excerpts, depending on a sustained structure for their effect.

Much ignored in his later years, and bypassed by the vagaries of literary fashion, his poems remain among the most individual and obsessively crafted of any written in English in the past half century.

REVIEWS

THE REVIEW PAGES

Writing for the Dead

STEPHEN ROMER ON THE PRAISE AND VITUPERATION OF GEOFFREY HILL

GEOFFREY HILL
The Triumph of Love
Penguin, £8.99
ISBN 0 140 58910 4

THE TRIUMPH OF LOVE is Geoffrey Hill's seventh individual collection. It is, if you like, the seventh candle on his Hannukah candelabrum of witness. Following closely, by his standards, after *Canaan* (1996), it is an extraordinary and bewildering book and one which creates a profound unease. In what he calls this "maze" of his "own devising", *The Triumph of Love* is a single, free-standing poem divided into 150 sections, a resurrection of a form of rhetoric (he tells us) that was known as *laus et vituperatio*, praise and vituperation. Throughout it, Hill revisits his major themes, his self-styled "obsessions", singling out certain great figures or events of language for praise, but more often heaping vituperation upon his own century, its wars and atrocities, its "compleasance" with political lies, its cultural amnesia, its failure to honour the dead or to bear witness. Following Leopardi, it is also explicitly Hill's *A se stesso*: "*Dispera l'ultima volta*" – despair for the last time, says the Italian poet to himself, confronted with "*l'infinità vanita del tutto*". There are manifold signs of finality, or at least of summation in this great outcry of Hill's, as he rounds snarlingly on himself, but more snarlingly upon his detractors and the "contemporary scene" in general. "What remains? You may well ask"; "Grief – now, after sixty years" – such phrases set the elegiac tone, but Hill remains embattled; and as never before, in *The Triumph of Love* he bares his wounds.

It is, and is designed to be, a provocative book – beginning with the title. Love is indeed an "unfamiliar name" to be associated with so much anger and bitterness. It is easy to dislike Hill, for his parade of erudition, for his distrust, even contempt, or what, in his own words, "is dangerously and equivocally termed the reading public", for his hectoring *de haut en bas* preachiness, for his cultivated aloofness. Even his admirers, among whom I count myself, are likely to be lambasted as sycophants – "the applause of self-styled his peers" is a discomfiting phrase that comes to mind. And in this latest book he seems to revel in the resentment he inspires – section XXXIX is typical:

Rancorous, narcissistic old sod – what
makes him go on? We thought, hoped rather,
he might be dead. Too bad. So how
much more does he have of injury time?

This biting demotic – which jostles with beautifully turned passages of theological argument, biblical grandiloquence, exact description of landscape – is only part of what makes the poem so bewildering, and even shocking in its brutal parataxis. The epigraph, from Nehemiah, reads "And I sent messengers unto them, saying, I am doing a great worke, so that I can not come down: why should the worke cease, whilest I leave it, and come downe to you?" It is repeated in four languages: Hebrew, Latin, German and English. Hill's epigraphs are always fraught with meaning, and this is no exception. We should be in no doubt that it is also Hill himself who is engaged on a "great worke" and he it is who does "come down" in this book, at times, to "explain himself", frequently in outbursts of spleen and bad-temper. How else explain the frequent interpolations of "ED" – a hectoring voice that "explains" some of his allusions, as in this from CXXV: "*praecedentem tempore et natura* [Strewth!!! / 'already present in time as in nature'? – ED]". One of the major problems I have with this book lies in the uneasiness of the humour, or in the uncertainty of the tone. If this is meant to be funny (by no means sure) then it does not work; if it isn't, the manifest impatience of the tone is insulting to the reader. One of Hill's many resentments against his critics resides in their failure to recognize his humour – and there is humour in his work (the marvellous sequence from *King Log*, 'The Songbook of Sebastian Arrurruz' would be a good example.) But in *The Triumph of Love* the humour is almost raucous, and comes with a disheartening snarl.

Yes, it is easy to resent Hill. He himself, in his interludes of *A se stesso*, catalogues some of the reasons, his learning for instance (never lightly worn):

> Shameless old man, bent on committing
> more public nuisance. Incontinent
> fury wetting the air. Impotently
> bereft satire. Charged with erudition,
> put up by the defence to be his own accuser.
>
> (XXXVII)

The word-play on "charged" is typical; he is both fraught with, and accused of – erudition. These interpolations – *A se stesso*, "ED" and a trio of invented critics who put him angrily on his mettle throughout the book, "Croker", "MacSikker" and "O'Shem" – represent what he calls in one of his essays the "antiphonal voice of the heckler". In part they are there for dramatic effect, they create a "dialogic" texture in the work but do they really make any difference? Does Hill really repent of his erudition, of his obscure allusions? Is he in any way chastened? To adopt his own demotic: like hell he is. It is the emptiness of the gesture, and, as I have noted, the uncertainty of the tone, that is at first sight dismaying in this poem. It is not the erudition *per se* that presents a problem (unless, that is, you do not regard poetry as a "learned art", and that Eliot or Pound's hammering on about the importance of acquiring "the tradition" is an irrelevance). The fact that to read *The Triumph of Love* properly entails amassing a small library around one (the Bible, the Latin poets, the *stilnovisti*, the Neo-Platonists, More, Milton, Hobbes, Blake, Wordsworth, Coleridge, Pound to name but a few) is probably to be welcomed. The problem resides rather in Hill's gnostic approach to knowledge, as the possession of a select group of initiates, (Professors of Moral Theology, say) and the complacency that comes with that view. Where is Hill's *ABC of Reading*? Pound's earnest wish was to educate: with Hill I am not so sure. What are we to make of a passage like this, for example, a knowing aside from the lecture podium:

> I should hold for my own, my self-giving,
> my retort upon Emerson's "alienated majesty",

> the *De Causa Dei* of Thomas Bradwardine.
>
> (VIII)

Here I must confess to my own ignorance, but the presence of those first-person possessives discourages me from scurrying off to look up Bradwardine in the library.

It is crucial to deal with this question of erudition, of the learned allusion because, I suspect, it is the "dragon in the gate" that bars many from enjoyment of Hill's finest work. It is also absolutely central to his major theme as a poet – as expressed in his often-quoted belief that "in handling the English language the poet makes an act of recognition that etymology is history. The history of the creation and the debasement of words is a paradigm of the loss of the kingdom of innocence and original justice". It is also the key to Hill's involvement with the writings of the past – his championing, in this poem, of, among others, Milton's political pamphlets, or of Wordsworth's two Prefaces and his "great tract on the Convention of Cintra" (LXX), examples, he says, of "Active virtue: that which shall contain / Its own passion in the public weal". Eliot put the matter resoundingly in his famous essay on tradition when he said of the dead writers that "they are that which we know". Hill, at his worst, alludes like a scatter-gun; he is at his best when allusion (whether made explicitly or not) is integrated and springs out of an image or a metaphor – as in this beautiful passage about his (remembered) childhood:

> So what is faith if it is not
> inescapable endurance? Unrevisited, the ferns
> are breast-high, head-high, the days
> lustrous, with their hinterlands of thunder.
> Light is this instant, far-seeing
> into itself, its own
> signature on things that recognize
> salvation. I
> am an old man, a child, the horizon
> is Traherne's country.
>
> (CXXI)

The name of Traherne brings into focus the cloud of reminiscences from the religious Metaphysicals, but something of Eliot's visionary lines on Simeon are present too, and doubtless there are others. Yet Hill has made them his own, has personalized these allusions: our reading is enriched by the echoes, not impoverished. Few poets can match Hill when he is writing out of the tradition like this – a tradition focused and dependent upon a certain exactitude of natural description. The same almost visionary intensity, again related to childhood, is present in LIII:

> Leave it now, leave it; give it over
> to that all-gathering general English light,
> in which each separate bead
> of drizzle at its own thorn-tip stands
> as revelation.

These sections create organic links with earlier poems of his, the descriptions of landscape in *Tenebrae*, section 5 of the Péguy poem, or the 'Parentalia' poems of Canaan where we find, unforgettably: "The things of earth snagging the things of grace, / darkened hawthorn, its late flare…". Despite the *gravitas* of his poems of historical witness, I am not sure that it isn't as a poet of landscape – in the rich Wordsworthian or Coleridgean sense of its being mysteriously cognate with the mind's own processes of self-realization – that Hill chiefly excels.

But as *The Triumph of Love* makes abundantly clear, Hill's huge ambition (as he might say, his "vocation") could never allow him to rest content with being a "mere" poet of landscape. In this collection he demands to be taken seriously as a social and political satirist, as a moralist, as a scourge of the age, as – always – a "witness for the witness". The landscape itself, or the "moral landscape", now seems to him a "metamorphic rock- / strata, in which particular grace, / individual love, decency, endurance, / are traceable across the faults" (LI). Landscape, that is, provides more than stretches of freedom, of untrammelled vision, but is identified with those qualities he prizes in his heroes, from the Catholic poet-martyrs all the way through to those exemplary figures of resistance in our own century – "Moltke, the two Boenhoeffers, von Haeften" (CXLII) – and one might add the poets who held fast against political lies – Mandelstam, Celan, Montale. And, by now almost emblematic of his work, the collective suffering of the Jewish people, in its extended historical perspective. But herein also lies Hill's personal drama as a poet: he was not there, he can only ever be a "latecomer". This sense of somehow having "missed out" on an age that forged martyrs and heroes haunts his work from the beginning. In *King Log*, the Battle of Towton

"commands one's belated witness" he says in a note. Addressing Mandelstam he laments how "The dead keep their sealed lives / And again I am too late". In the new book, he gives way to a splenetic outburst against "Croker", one of his invented critics (named after the Croker who damned Keats's 'Endymion'?): "Confound you, Croker – you and your righteous /censure! I have admitted, many times, / my absence from the salient, from the coal-face / in Combs Pit, Thornhill.[...] My cowardice / is not contested. I am saying (simply) / what is to become of memory?" (CXXXVIII). But Croker has a point – there is something problematic about Hill's yearning for "the Bloody Question" of the Catholic recusants: "we have lost the Bloody Question" he says in CXLII, or if we haven't "Less hangs on the outcome, / or by, or around it". His yearning is similar to Eliot lamenting the passing of an age in which a man could be – theologically speaking – damned. What Hill cannot stand seems to be "consensus" of any kind, however benevolent, which elides in his imagination with time-serving sycophancy and the "fashionable" whether in politics or in aesthetics: "Take accessible to mean / acceptable, accommodating, openly servile" (XL). His despair goes deep, as here:

> What remains? You may well ask. Construction
> or deconstruction? There is some poor
> mimicry of choice, whether you build or destroy.
> But the Psalms – they remain;…
> (XXIII)

Deconstruction: the dismantling of an author's intentionality, the denial of a continuous subject, language as an autonomous entity – it's hard to think of a critical concept that would strike such death to the heart of a poet like Hill, for whom the acts and statements of individuals in very specific historical contexts are sacrosanct. It sets him at absolutely the opposite pole from a poet like John Ashbery, say. Or even from the nameless "Swedish millionaires" "N and N" – recent Nobel prizewinning poets, presumably, whom he derides, in one of the most unattractive (and unjustified) outbursts in the book: "I / write for the dead; N.N for the living / dead" (CIV). The gruesome joke of the enjambment, combined with the tone, is an example of Hill at his worst in this poem.

That needs saying, even though I am on the whole in sympathy with Hill's poetics. In a period that George Steiner has described as the "twilight of the humanities", here is a poet who does not shrink from affirming that "poetry is a form of responsible behaviour", or that "in the act of refining technique one is not only refining emotion, one is also constantly defining and redefining one's ethical and moral sensibility" (in his interview with John Haffenden). In *The Triumph of Love*, certain passages of dramatically re-imagined historical witness are, no less so than in his previous books, remarkable achievements. In section XX, for example, his conflation of the furnace in the Book of Daniel, with footage from, presumably, the destruction of the Warsaw ghetto is shockingly strong, and touched with genius. But here again, I am deeply uneasy with the form, or "continuum", of his new poem: he rehearses his "obsessions" – the Holocaust among them – as parts of his "personality", for that is finally what the "spienetics" and the *A se stesso* interludes draw attention to. Extraordinarily, for a poet so hypersensitive to such questions, *The Triumph of Love* – from this distance at least, it takes time to come to a final judgement on such a complex work – seems in this regard to constitute a lapse of taste, an example of great gifts gone awry.

Subjects Matter

by David Wheatley

PHILIP GROSS
The Wasting Game
Bloodaxe, £6.95
ISBN 1 85224 479 8

JO SHAPCOTT
My Life Asleep
Oxford Poets, £6.99
ISBN 0 19 288 107 5

FRED D'AGUIAR
Bill of Rights
Chatto, £7.99
ISBN 0 7011 6525 1

ROBERT CRAWFORD
Spirit Machines
Cape, £8.00
ISBN 0 224 05901 7

STEPHEN ROMER
Tribute
Oxford Poets, £7.99
ISBN 0 19 2888 104 3

WHERE DO STORIES come from? In one of Roald Dahl's *Tales of the Unexpected* a man takes a wrong turning off a motorway and finds a factory that manufactures jokes and urban myths. Having discovered this secret the interloper is promptly killed. While it would be too fanciful to think of a factory somewhere off the M6 churning out themes for contemporary poetry, it's hard to read any amount of slim volumes without noticing the same few subjects cropping up again and again. "Anything, however small, may make a poem; nothing, however great, is certain to", Edward Thomas wrote, but the belief that some subjects are inherently more poetic than others stubbornly persists. There is the old fogey variant, as when Larkin complained about judging the Arvon Poetry Competition because the organizers had "chucked out" all the poems about "love and nature" he would have liked. On the cynical side, *The Printer's Devil* used to publish blacklists of subjects for poems (spiritual uplift in cathedrals, wars seen on television etc.). Despite the wisdom of Thomas's statement then, subject matter is important. At its best, in breakthrough collections like Plath's *Ariel*, new subjects are part of a writer's discovering a whole new language. At its worst, the same old subjects are asses dragging their cartloads of poems behind them off to the knacker's yard of literary history.

The five collections under review here are about, variously, a young woman's struggle with anorexia, the erotic metamorphoses of the female imagination, a religious cult which ends up committing mass suicide, the meshing of the emotional, the spiritual and the technological in modern life, and falling out and in of love in a package holiday's worth of European cities. The first sounds familiar, except that it's written not from the woman's perspective, but that of her father. Unusual takes on familiar subjects are themselves a stock device since Martianism, so without awarding any plaudits in advance for subversion of our jaded expectations let's see what's new or otherwise about these five books.

Philip Gross's *The Wasting Game* isn't all about anorexia, though the title poem and a number of others on the same subject in the first pages take some getting past. Noting the speedbumps and "Caution Patients Crossing" sign in the hospital driveway and the "sobbing on legs" he passes in the corridor, the poet visits his daughter only to find "her silence is a waiting room". The language in 'The Wasting Game' reeks of Plath, but the fact that it is spoken to rather than by the anorexic girl deflects it from being parodic of that dangerously powerful influence. "She tries hissing herself offstage", Gross tells us, describing the theatricality of it all: eating disorder as self-directed performance art. The musical setting for lines like these would have to be *Death and the Maiden*:

> I could hate
>
> those frail maids fading beautifully
> in books, wax lilies, pale-succulent
>
> stalks that might snap
> at a touch. The bird-dropping of blood
>
> in a lace-bordered handkerchief
> like the monstrance on the nuptual sheet.
>
> A consummation most devoutly wished
> by death.

Thankfully the girl never gets hung up about her surname, but "gross"-ly intrusive or exploitative 'The Wasting Game' is not.

Since Christopher Reid's 1985 collection named after her, the spirit of Katerina Brac inevitably accompanies any English poet at large in Eastern Europe. With his Estonian Devonian pedigree Philip Gross carries this baggage lightly, and 'A Liminal State', about a visit to Tallinn in 1994, is an accomplished piece of reportage. If subject matter is important in poems so are facts, and Gross is perkily informative: we learn the fate of all those toppled statues of Lenin, Estonian tastes in daytime TV, and that post from Moscow to Tallinn goes faster via London these days. In a very different style is 'The Language of the Bird People', which explores transmigration, the idea of north, and the origins of writing in a Finno-Ugric tribe: the aleatory beginning and anthropological style are almost Prynnean. Mixed in with the randomness are some bull's eyes of metaphors and similes: a handshake is "a brisk clunk /like a gear change", a lift in its glass tube is "snug as the plunger in a hypodermic".

Plath returns in 'That Grave, Heptonstall Churchyard'. Sylvia Plath's grave has to be at the top of anyone's blacklist of embarrassing subjects for poems, but again Gross defies the odds. After some play with the phrase "in place" (the finality of death has put her "in her place"), and the fact that the poem's addressee is also American, he concludes: "Does she belong? Do we? Where / else could these thoughts be at home but on / disputed ground?". Occasionally he drags a metaphor out too long, as in 'Hard Water', but *The Wasting Game* finds Philip Gross at a healthy remove from mid-career sag or sprawl.

Let me say straight away that I wasn't as convinced by Jo Shapcott's *My Life Asleep*, either in comparison to Gross's collection or on its own terms. Shapcott has edited an anthology devoted to how surprised poets have been by the modern world, but she handles her themes in a disappointingly predictable way, even (especially) when the theme is the subversion of the predictable. The title alone of 'Mrs Noah: Taken After the Flood' suggests an encore performance of a tune we've heard once too often from Carol Ann Duffy, and that's exactly what it is. Then there is 'The Mad Cow in Space' and 'The Mad Cow is Vogue Model', whose jaunty-twee tone wears thin very fast. The terse 'Pig', 'Hedgehog' and 'Rhinoceros' don't make a persuasive case for Shapcott as an animal-watcher: the short-circuiting of description into touching or witty but lightweight anecdote is very much the Shapcott vice.

What made 'Phrasebook' such a fine poem was the sense of the language moving beyond the control of the speaker. She tries it again in 'Motherland': "England. It hurts my lips to shape / the word. This country makes me say / too many things I can't say. Home / of me, myself, my motherland" (Marina Tsvetaeva's motherland that is, since it's a translation). This is a bit like not having your cake and not eating it too. Even in 'Quark', whose use of the word "bollocks" caused such consternation on the London Underground, Shapcott creates a talking subatomic particle only to make it sound like an e-popping teenage clubber. The exotic is made to sound like the familiar, rather than the other way round ("You're inclined to confuse / me with yourself", as the speaker says in 'Les Roses').

Her best images tend to be of unabashed carnality, like her Brünhilde with "her instinct for the / most vivid ways to ripen, / the most vivid ways to rot". Despite that Wagnerian name, Shapcott doesn't go in for anything operatic or on too grand a scale; karoake or a pub sing-along is much more her thing. This means that her poems are never lacking in warm sociability, but also that they often fall prey to what Christopher Ricks memorably called the "halitosis of bonhomie". Finally, there is the nagging sense that minus its translations from Enzensberger, Tsvetaeva and a longish sequence from Rilke's French, *My Life Asleep* is too skimpy for it is own good. If only Shapcott had written more poems like 'Letter to Dennis', which manages to be more believable in a few lines than all those mad cows and unconvincingly recycled Greek myths:

> Still rude, I hope, still raucous and rejoicing
> in the most painful erection in heaven
> which rises through its carapace of sores
> and cracking skin to sing in English.
>
> You are as live to me as the tongue
> in my mouth, as the complicated shame
> of Englishness. Would you call me lass?
> Would you heave up any stars for my crown?

A collection of misfits leaves the Old World for America led by a charismatic leader and high on utopian spirituality. On arrival things go wrong, personalities clash, drugs are taken, sexual intrigue is rife, and it all ends in wholesale slaughter. It sounds like the plot of Muldoon's *Madoc* but is in fact Fred D'Aguiar's *Bill of Rights*. It tells the story of the Jonestown mass suicide in 1978, when over nine hundred people died drinking cyanide on the instructions of failed Messiah Jim Jones.

Bill of Rights is a narrative poem, but like *Madoc* it doesn't have the stamina to come out as one continuous block of text, certainly not in the manner of Les Murray's *Fredy Neptune*. Instead it's written in short (usually page-long) units, many of which end with a passage in italics where D'Aguiar indulges his taste for litany and nursery rhyme of a sort. These show the narrator suffering from a mixture of religious mania and suggestibility, the swirling language of his prayers finding all too ready an echo in Jim Jones's demented oratory. In many ways these passages are the testing ground for the madness that breaks out later on, by which time the stereo effect of the italics is no longer required.

It isn't all just mania and violence though. Stray references to Yoknapatawpha County and the "performance poetry circuit" hint that the narrator may not be quite the trollish simpleton we've taken him for, and before long he's cracking jokes about Derek Mahon, Tom Paulin, parodying Simon Armitage's 'A Week and a Fortnight' and putting 'Descartes before the Hobbes'. A key stage in the narrator's disillusion is his discovery of Jones's sexual and narcotic decadence. If this shows his leader up as a fraud, it also encourages the narrator to act out his violent impulses in what are now increasingly anarchic conditions (his hymns to his Uzi rifle are just as ecstatic as any to God):

> Jim Jones in his heaven.
> A gross of virgins
> Impregnated by him,
> Lie dead and swollen,
> With child.
>   Dead
> And swollen people
> Scattered everywhere.
> Jim Jones in his heaven.
> Him Temple haunted
> By a thousand ghosts.

As these lines show the sex too in *Bill of Rights* is fairly grotesque, another trick borrowed from Muldoon. So is D'Aguiar's use of the refrain (compare the choruses in *Shining Brow*) and, since we're on the subject, even the naming of one of the characters (Muldoon's 'Yarrow' has an 'S—', Bill of Rights an 'L—'). It's all too much to be a coincidence: could there possibly be a subtext that Muldoon exercises a shamanic hold on D'Aguiar's generation not unlike that of a charismatic leader like… no, not Jim Jones, but you see my point. If so, perhaps this constitutes D'Aguiar's simultaneous act of homage and exorcism. On balance though, what he takes from the Irishman he puts to good use. As the complex work it is, *Bill of Rights* doesn't lend itself to byte-sized quotations, but the lasting impression is of a skilful and successful book-length narrative poem, and how often does one of those come along?

Robert Crawford's *Spirit Machines* is divided between the impulse to write heartfelt elegies and poems about his childhood, and the urge to duck out of the whole lyric thing and into the poetic equivalent of virtual reality. It's a dilemma he solves by making technology a governing theme of the book, especially in the poems about his father and his work in a bank. 'Time and Motion' contrasts the old decency of Edwardian Scotland, where even the words 'time is money' seem quaintly relaxed, with the instantaneous world of fibre-optics and e-mail. Crawford prevents us from making the lazy equation of the past with lost authenticity in a poem like 'CD Rom', whose read-only memory imbues a collection of crucial sounds (a soprano's top C, saying 'I do') with a new form of what Walter Benjamin called "aura": "Throwaway, absolute, unremixable, // Teasing the rapt ear forever". Crawford is fascinated by the processes of transmission and exchange, which he sees as unifying the sacred and the worldly. Wallace Stevens's adage that "Money is a kind of poetry" still raises eyebrows, but in 'Exchange' Crawford goes further: "Promising always to pay the bearer, money aspires to the condition of purest spirit".

The comparison with Stevens only goes so far, however. Crawford's overtly nationalist concerns are never very far away, as you'd expect from someone who once dedicated a book "To Scotland". It's a pity then that 'A Result', on the Scottish devolution vote, should end with such a weakly Heaneyesque cadence. Similarly, litanies of Scottish place names ('Grim Reaper', 'Old Tunnockians') don't look very original since Paterson's trainspotting in *God's Gift to Women*, and 'Bereavement' too comes very much courtesy of the Dundonian's '11:00: Baldovan' (which in turn was ripped off from MacNeice's 'Soap Suds'). Questions of attribution and subjectivity are made to look more difficult in a world where, good postmodernists that we are, "There is no here. Here goes" ('Alford'), but the effect of Crawford's poetry isn't remotely as disorienting as that of a true experimentalist like Prynne, to drag him into it again. The information technology, in other words, conceals an unashamedly humanist and even conventional sensibility.

Crawford's attempts at balladeering in 'Highland Poems' don't do much for me: as a piece of nationalist rhetoric 'The Ballad of Wendy Wood' has a long way to go to catch up with Yeats's 'Roger Casement' or 'The O'Rahilly'. His ludic pieces are effective as far as they go. The title of 'A Life-Exam' promises revelations, but confines itself to list of seventy-one questions. "Rewrite The Waste Land using only / English words of one syllable" asks number one, though by the end of the exam I was doodling inattentively in the margins. The enjoyable 360-line 'Impossibility' is devoted to the "anti-syzygously Scottish" nineteenth-century writer Margaret Oliphant. One last example of the perils of transmission comes in 'Liglag' where the repeated words "Tine haert, tine a'" are translated "If you let sorrow overcome you, you lose everything". The best poems in *Spirit Machines* – 'The Descent', 'Relief', 'Liglag' and 'Alford' – are those where the technology theme deepens the sense of loss rather than affirmatively spiriting it away. In the words of question seventeen from 'A Life-Exam': "Act on this".

Of this batch of five poets, Stephen Romer shows the closest thing to a belief in lyric as impassioned, brief utterance. In the course of *Tribute*, his third collection, a relationship breaks down, and there's never any doubt that this really is loss and not something being experienced on a CD Rom. Technology makes an appearance in 'Functionary', where it forms part of the anonymous world a bureaucrat frets to exchange for "the philosophies of natural being". Making allowances for the bureaucrat's willingness to resort to a cliché like this, Romer's seriousness and classical manner are refreshingly untempted by the subversion and simulacra we find in Shapcott and Crawford. *Tribute* contains both epigraphs and a translation from Montale, and at times comes close to the tone of thrilling erotic distress perfected by the Italian in his *Motetti*. 'Necessity' ends: "such is the process, / casting wide its net, // though even now, / Necessity! you have no use for us" (the positioning of that exclamation mark is inspired). In 'Oriole' the call of the bird 'didla-didlio' returns at the end of the poem as 'Daedalio…', suggesting the innocent scene he has just described ('your nakedness and mine') is in reality a complex labyrinth.

Tribute enjoys its polyglot cosmopolitanism: in Italy a *primavera* breeze blows 'spring in every language', '*Arbbre de bhoneur*' plays with misspellings in French and '*Przy-przy*' finds domestic happiness in the pronunciation of a Polish consonant. The theme is love, that 'Terrible

REVIEWS

Crystallization' of the Platonic ideal in the particular. It would be easy to detach overwrought or awkward lines from poems like 'Suddenly', 'Fallacy' or 'Laura', but Romer's poems work cumulatively, toying with a romantic illusion on one page only to tear it to shreds on the next. "One cannot lose what one has not possessed", Geoffrey Hill wrote in 'The Songbook of Sebastian Arrurruz', and among Romer's best passages are those where he picks morosely at the scab of absence. 'A Lesson in Materialism' recounts Diderot's wish as a strict atheist for his 'particles' to mix with those of his beloved after death in 'atomic disaggregation'. Romer adds:

> We too have undergone
> a change; and, prematurely single,
>
> tender traces are all I have
> (being forced to disassemble you
> into everything else that I love).

Like the exclamation mark in 'Necessity', those brackets decorously register the poet's scruple. 'Disassemble' echoes 'dissemble', suggesting the hopelessness of his attempts to find the beloved everywhere else but in person. 'Ideal' moves backwards from fragments of memory ("what is left me...") to a deeper scepticism about the reality he hopes to recapture, remembering sand between the woman's toes on the beach and "your castle engulfed already like this island / perhaps we never sailed to". Other fine poems in this vein deserving a mention are 'Chakra' and 'Monumental Buddha'.

By the third section Romer has moved on to more discursive travel poems, usually with a favourite writer (Nerval, Pushkin, Mandelstam) somewhere in the background. The recapturing of his "mammal's peace / between your neck and shoulders" in 'Hibernation' helps to make the end of *Tribute* more easygoing than its beginning, though without the intensity of the earlier sections. This is not Romer's *For Lizzie and Harriet* or *The Dolphin* then: much as he tries to keep up the self-excoriation, cheerfulness keeps breaking through. If he goes on from here to write about it with the same intensity he brings to unhappiness, the sad, searching and elegant poems of the first half of *Tribute* will have been more than worthwhile.

Life in the Bus Lane

By Kate Clanchy

RITA DOVE
On the Bus with Rosa Parks
Norton, £10.95
ISBN 0 393 04722 9

RITA DOVE IS to the poetry of Black America as Toni Morrison is to its prose: the intellectual, the re-mythologiser, the internationally-respected multiple laureate. Her new collection *On the Bus with Rosa Parks* has, like Morrison's recent work, an air of gracious calm. Dove is now free of the exploratory restlessness which characterised her early work: she is centred, and certain of her powers. As she puts it in last poem of this collection: her "heart, too, / has come down to earth; Where I'm at now / is more like riding a bus / through unfamiliar neighbourhoods – / chair in recline, the view chopped square".

The "neighbourhoods" she rides through, though, are not "unfamiliar" to admirers of Dove's work. In 'Cameos', the sequence of poems which opens the volume, Dove returns to the America of the 'twenties and 'thirties, the era of Thomas and Beulah, her ground-breaking collection about the life of her grandparents. In a series of askance, quirky, perfectly-observed vignettes she gives us the lives and complex relationships of a black family living – as Morrison's characters do – with racism and their painful moment of history, without being defined by them. The sequence is a tremendous pleasure to read – tense as a novel, but at once more ambiguous and more focused. Dove's lyric voice has matured to the point where, effortlessly, without ever stepping outside the demotic, she can give every voice its own tune: thus Lucille

> among the flamingos
> is pregnant; is pained
> because she cannot stoop to pluck

REVIEWS

>   the plumpest green tomato
>   deep on the crusted vine

The patterning of plosives and assonances invade the mundane scene (the flamingos are plastic) as certainly as the thoughts of eggs, her child, food and her errant lover Joe do her thoughts. Meanwhile, elsewhere, Joe clicks out a simpler blues, his insouciance belied by the repeating 'O's:

> Joe knows somewhere
> he has a father
> who would have told
>   him
> how to act. Mama,
> stout as a yellow turnip,
> loved to bewail her wild
>   good luck:
> Black foot Injun, with
> hair like a whip.

This elegant control allows for equally elegant ironies: the son Lucille bears both kills fireflies and is the aspiring intellectual of the family, despises both his racist textbook and his inadequate father, is at once the future and the nemesis of his family. His education teaches him to think in Latinate terms, to measure out his hopes in chilly fricatives and sibilants,

>   Better
>   the clear incurious drip
>   of fluid from pipet
>   to reassuring beaker...
>
>   Most of all
>   He'd like to study
>   the composition of the stars.

There are more familiar Dove "neighbourhoods" in the central sections of the collection: we revisit the passionate, bookish, childhood which Dove outlined in 'The Yellow House on the Corner' in the poems of *Freedom: A Bird's Eye View* resume the exotic wandering of Museum in many of the poems of Black on a Saturday Night and find

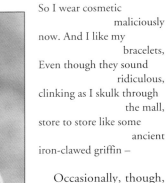

new meditations to add to the lyrics on generation, motherhood and family of her most recent collection, Mother Love in 'Revenant'. Generally, these poems make for welcome additions to Dove's *oeuvre*: extending her territory a little, demonstrating the grand reach of that relaxed voice in her accounts of Saint Veronica and the Venus of Willendorf, and the enduring strength of her personal lyric in poems such as '*Gotterdammerung*' which musically and subtly celebrates ageing:

> So I wear cosmetic
>   maliciously
> now. And I like my
>   bracelets,
> Even though they sound
>   ridiculous,
> clinking as I skulk through
>   the mall,
> store to store like some
>   ancient
> iron-clawed griffin –

Occasionally, though, Dove seems to be repeating her early themes without her early force, and even to fall into that vice of the truly grand: sententiousness. One of Dove's first-published poems, 'Geometry', famously and thrillingly captured the early stages of intellectual development by enacting a series of magical transformations around the child protagonist. 'Singsong'. and 'Testimonial' in this volume seem, by contrast, to conventionalise and sentimentalise Dove's child-self who is described as 'tongued in honey and coddled in milk' and as being 'pirouette and flourish', 'filigree and flame' and 'older than I am today'. 'The First Book' even abandons Dove's subtle sound schemes and resorts to cliché in its anxiety to get its message over: "Open it. / Go ahead, it won't bite. / Well... maybe a little. / More a nip like. A tingle. / It's pleasurable really".

There is nothing, however, careless or sententious in the eponymous series of poems as the end of the book, which are given over to exploring and celebrating Rosa Parks' historic 1955 refusal to give up her bus seat to a white passenger. The poem's are acute, wide-ranging, well-researched, and, at their best, fully combine Dove's dazzling intellect with her lyric gift. 'The Situation is Intolerable', for example, starts as a reasonably conventional protest poem against the use of vague, Latinate, oppressive white language, then rapidly transforms itself, as the protester speaker asks us to consider, beyond "the perimeter in flames" the stars, which he configures as both Christian "missionaries" and as the jewels of an unseen, vast, black God:

> tiny, missionary stars –
> on high, serene, studding
> the inky brow of heaven.

Dove succeeds in giving equally rich voices to two of the lesser known protesters of the early Civil Rights movement, and in evoking the 'cloud cover / and germy air' of the scarred and dangerous Deep South. Ironically, Dove does not quite succeed in celebrating Rosa Parks herself. Her description of Parks today is, while adoring, curiously lacking in the particular details which illuminate the crowd around her. Similarly, the poem 'Rosa' consists of some quiet exterior details, and then, instead of a clarifying, central observation, a cliché: "the clean flame of her gaze". A little critical distance and the screen of fiction, we gather, is what allows Rita Dove to create her astonishing voices. She is at her best, as she rightly says, observing the world from her own seat on the bus.

Talking Books

by Ian McMillan

THE POETRY QUARTETS

1 Simon Armitage, Kathleen Jamie, Jackie Kay, Glyn Maxwell
ISBN 1 85224 468 3

2 Fleur Adcock, Carol Ann Duffy, Selima Hill, Carol Rumens
ISBN 1 85224 469 0

3 James Fenton, Tony Harrison, Peter Reading, Ken Smith
ISBN 1 85224 470 4
Bloodaxe, all £11.75

I MUST ADMIT that I'm a late arrival at the audiobooks ball; I do know they're immensely popular, and I recently did a little tour introducing actors who worked on audiobooks to audiences in libraries and I got a glimpse into a medium-sized but fully-developed world.

I realise that these aren't quite audiobooks; they're readings, with introductions and comments by the poets themselves, but they're meant to be listened to in the same way that audiobooks are, whilst ironing, in the car (don't lose the comma), in bed, whilst chopping carrots (don't lose the comma).

Each *Quartet* is two hours long, each poet getting roughly half an hour to read and talk about a number of poems, often old favourites, sometimes new poems. Simon Armitage reads from his sequence 'The Whole Of The Sky' from *Cloudcuckooland*, Peter Reading reads some very old poems and also some from his new collection *Ob*. Any listener coming to these poems for the first time would end up with a good, if incomplete (and that's the idea) map of current British Poetry.

Each *Quartet* has a kind of group identity: *Quartet One* is Youngish Turks, *Quartet Two* is Women, *Quartet Three* is Grand Oldish Men.

Quartet One is the liveliest and for me the best; Simon Armitage's voice is a large part of the enjoyment of his work; I like the *Cloudcuckooland* Poems, and Armitage's gentle Marsden tones set them off perfectly. It's the same with Kathleen Jamie; superb poems like 'The Tay Moses' and 'Crossing the Loch' are given extra dimensions by her Scots voice. Jackie Kay is a superb reader, of course, and although she's reined in a bit by the fact that the poems were recorded in her house (something I'll come back to later) her energy transcends the sofas and the wallpaper and the person sitting holding the mike, and poems like 'Brendon Gallacher' crackle with energy. Glyn Maxwell's poems are really designed to be heard, and it's great to hear them, even when you're chopping carrots.

REVIEWS

Quartet Two somehow captures a sense of intimate occasion, with all the poets doing the thing that audiobooks do best: speaking directly into the listener's ear, making you feel that you're on an *à-deux* picnic with the author, rathing than sharing them with a number of other coughers and nodders at a reading. Fleur Adcock's poems certainly crackle into lapidary focus when she reads them, the ghost of her New Zealand accent nudging the poems sharply into life; Carol Ann Duffy's voice is perfect for her poems and it would be hard to imagine them read by an actor; Selima Hill's and Carol Rumens' readings illuminate poems that have been a bit misty for me on the page, and that's a ringing endorsement for these cassettes, if one was needed.

My wife came in when I was listening to *Quartet Three* and she said she thought I was listening to a Party Political Broadcast, and it's true that even poets like Peter Reading and Tony Harrison can sound a bit, well, Radio 4, with only the voice to go on. This raises the question of who the audence is for these cassettes, and I think they really work best if you know the poems already. GCSE-takers, like my eldest daughter, studying the poems of Armitage and Duffy, will get that extra dimension from hearing the words spoken. On the other hand, people who are coming to these poems for the first time will, I think, need the poems in front of them, and of course that's no bad thing.

I said I'd come back to the house and here I am; almost all the poets here were recorded in their homes (all except Glyn Maxwell who was recorded in a London studio) and although we gain here in intimacy, we lose the Factor X that an audience, no matter how small, provides. I'm not suggesting that these cassettes should be like Billy Connolly Live Albums, but I think that when a poem is read aloud in front of an audience, the audience completes the continuum of the creativity that the poet starts. It could be that I'm completing that continuum listening to the poem while doing the ironing, but I'm not sure. Also I know that the cassettes are meant to be about the poems and nothing but the poems, but I feel that an opportunity was missed to make radio programmes: the poems could have been recorded in other settings; music and effects could have been used (sparingly) and the idea of a collection of poems on a cassette could have been made into an exciting and innovative thing.

That's only a small complaint, though: it's very good to have these quartets as the beginning of something. They are invaluable aids to study, to understanding; they're tasters for the work, and they teach the listener how to listen for the music in poems, for the rhythms, for the shiny flickerings behind the simple meanings of words, the flickerings that contain Poetry with a capital P.

One last thing: I'm not a particularly lusty opener of cassette boxes, and I know I'm eager and a bit clumsy, but each of these three boxes exploded in my hands as I tried to get into them and they're now useless bits of plastic. So open them carefully as though they're treasure, and they'll reward you.

Heartbreaking but also Very Funny

By Sheenagh Pugh

LOUISE GLÜCK
Meadowlands
Carcanet, £6.95
ISBN 1 85754 350 5

THIS IS LOUISE Glück's first new collection since *The Wild Iris*, though in the meantime Carcanet had reissued her previous collections intact as *The First Five Books of Poems*. I thought *The Wild Iris* a stunning book, with an intensity and stillness about its language that made it instantly and permanently memorable. Some reviewers were dismissive, choosing to see it as arcadian and escapist (only if you are dim enough to think it concerns flowers in gardens, rather than religious belief).

Maybe they will find the subject matter of this – the dissolution of a marriage – more contemporary and "relevant". They will however have to come to terms with the underlying myth woven through it: the protracted, interrupted homeward journey of Odysseus to Penelope. Names change, people don't. Odysseus becomes the archetypal wandering husband, Penelope the wife who defines herself in terms of him, Circe the interloper who, if she doesn't actually cause the break-up, provides an impetus for it and Telemachus the child of a breaking marriage who needs to accept that his parents' problems are not his. His voice, commenting wryly from the fringes of this relationship, is often the most compelling, as when he debates what to put on their tombstone:

> they are
> my parents, consequently
> I see them together,
> sometimes inclining to
> husband and wife, other times
> to opposing forces.
> ('Telemachus' Dilemma')

Telemachus' is not the only voice with a sense of humour and proportion, which may be why this collection is more readable than some poems on the same theme. There is resentment, but in the end a non-judgemental acceptance that it takes more than one person to wreck a relationship; grief at loss, but also a recognition that what was lost was also possessed and valued, if not for ever. In 'Parable of Flight', one partner (him, I think) likens a changing relationship to a migration;

> Does it matter where the birds go? Does it even
> matter
> what species they are?
> They leave here, that's the point,
> first their bodies, then their sad cries.
> And from that moment, cease to exist for us.
> You must learn to think of our passion that way.
> Each kiss was real, then
> each kiss left the face of the earth.

Early on, in 'Telemachus' Detachment', Telemachus says that as a child he found he parents' lives heartbreaking; now he finds them heartbreaking but also very funny. This paradox is captured perfectly in 'Ceremony', a conversation-poem between husband and wife in which each has an agenda; each is listening more to his or her own words than those of the other; questions and accusations are not answered, or are answered at some point far down the dialogue:

> One thing I've always hated
> about you: I hate that you refuse
> to have people at the house. Flaubert
> had more friends and Flaubert
> was a recluse.

> Flaubert was crazy; he lived
> with his mother.

> Living with you is like living
> at boarding school:
> chicken Monday, fish Tuesday.

> I have deep friendships
> I have friendships
> with other recluses.

> Why do you call it rigidity?
> Can't you call it a taste for
> ceremony? Or is your hunger for beauty
> completely satisfied by your own person?

> Another thing: name one other person
> who doesn't have furniture.

> We have fish Tuesday
> because it's fresh Tuesday. If I could drive
> we could have it different days.

The apparent inconsequentiality and littleness of the arguments is funny, but the humour accentuates rather than undermining the desperation and grief beneath.

There is the same intensity of language here as in *The Wild Iris*, but a rawer tone somehow, as befitting more human concerns. Sometimes statements of feeling are unexpectedly blunt and honest – as in "Circe's Grief", where the mistress makes herself known to the wife, on the ground that: "if I am in her head forever / I am in your life forever". Or 'Purple Bathing Suit', where one partner watches the other in increasing irritation:

> you are a small irritating purple thing
> and I would like to see you walk off the face of the
> earth
> because you are all that's wrong with my life
> and I need you and I claim you.

American poets seem more inclined to this emotional honesty than English ones, with their dread of sounding simple or sentimental and consequent habit of hiding behind irony where they don't have to take any risks. I think *The Wild Iris* is always going to be my favourite of hers, but at the end of this I felt, as then, that I had been somewhere that mattered and experienced something beyond word-play.

REVIEWS

Waiting for the World's Wife

by Helen Dunmore

CAROL ANN DUFFY
The Pamphlet
Anvil Press, £5.00
ISBN 0 85646 307 8

POETS HAVE BEEN much in the public eye this past year or so. But if their personalities have been analysed in the broadsheets, or blazoned across the tabloids, poems themselves have stayed in the shadows. Biography, not form, dominates the discussion, Poets are reduced to stereotypes, even though it was to find a new container for their thoughts, presumably, that they tried to write poetry in the first place. Ted Hughes' life and work are subsumed into The Ted and Sylvia Story, or into an idea of greatness which bypasses the poems themselves. Candidates for the laureateship are pitched to the public like film-scripts to sated Hollywood moguls. There's Tony Harrison: uncomfortably political, a royal refusnik, yet strangely capable of being one of the few poets in the country who makes an excellent living purely from his poetry. Seamus Heaney would be perfect, but for the colour of his passport. It is the dispositions of the poets, and their public postures, which are emphasised. The quality of their poetry becomes secondary. Can they make themselves agreeable, are they good on committees, would they say something unfortunate if introduced to Princess Margaret, are they black, white, British, Irish, male, female, heterosexual, homosexual? Slowly the reality emerges: poets are an awkward squad. Many don't want the job at all; others cannot be relied up to do it without subversion. In this market, Armitage becomes the meteoric young Yorkshireman; U. A. Fanthorpe the loveable eccentric. Derek Walcott features as magisterial Nobel figure, bookend to Heaney.

On it goes, and on, riddled with inaccuracies, empty of poetry. If this is the popularisation of poetry which we have all been encouraged to work towards, it is a great disappointment. Which newspaper has had the guts to print a poem by each of the poets under discussion, and let readers taste the work? Perhaps they are simply being realistic; most people prefer gossip to poetry.

Carol Ann Duffy, however, is a genuinely popular poet. Her work sells, is widely read, discussed, enjoyed, imitated. These simple facts bear some repetition, because although simple they are also very rare. Few poets ever manage to make their readers feel, again and again, that strange pang of mingled recognition and excitement that Duffy can evoke with such poems as 'Plainsong', 'Warming her Pearls', 'Small Female Skull' or 'The Way My Mother Speaks'. Her ear is fine, her tone beautifully poised, her language makes an appeal which seems to be naked but is really clothed in art: "Only tonight / I am happy and sad / like a child / who stood at the end of summer / and dipped a net / in a green erotic pond". Such work does not crumble away at a third reading, or indeed, at a thirtieth.

Carol Ann Duffy's new collection, *The Pamphlet*, comes six years after her last, *Mean Time*, which won both the Forward and the Whitbread Literary Prizes. *The Pamphlet* is a fair length for a pamphlet, at forty-eight pages (although the poems begin on page 9, according to a baffling convention of poetry publication). The first and longest poem in the pamphlet, 'Standing Stone', is a public poem written for the opening of the Museum of Scotland last year. It shows that Duffy is perfectly competent and at ease in writing such poetry. Commissioned poetry has to work hard not to flatter the expectations of those who commission it, and Duffy does not entirely succeed in keeping an edge on this poem. It's a little too comfortable in stringing together a history that will not disconcert the museum visitors too much. When 'Standing Stome' flares into imaginative life, it shows what might have been achieved:

> Davy MacLachlan stamped his mark
> on the Touchplate, to guarantee
> his good and faithful work, like a kiss,
> slung his coat over his shooder
> and whistled away into the New…

There's something to be said about the voicelessness into which public history has thrust most of our ancestors, but Duffy does not quite say it on this occasion. She is fully capable of doing so, as she has proved in many other poems. In 'Phone-in', for example, she took the anonymous figure of a woman trying to express her fear of violence and crime, her frightened sense that the country has changed. The poem is about banality and cliché, and yet it absolutely avoids patronising either its subject or its occasion.

'Standing Female Nude', again, took the concept of public poetry into new territory. The private, intimate relationship between model and artist was explored in all its wider resonances. Duffy brilliantly dramatised the way that women's bodies appear before the public and the private eye. Much of Duffy's work demonstrates that public poetry is most telling when most unexpected. But in 'Standing Stone' she is a little too careful in her handling of national pieties. The poem has none of the originality Kathleen Jamie achieves on a similar theme, in 'Mr and Mrs Scotland are Dead'. But then, would the Museum of Scotland have wanted Jamie's poem for the occasion of its opening?

Carol Ann Duffy's poetry has always reflected a strong sense of the tension between being inside and being outside, and indeed between being an insider and an outsider. Her love poetry is sharpened by a sense of fragility. At any moment, the bliss of being one of love's insiders can be destroyed. Love is a home, and the loveless are homeless, wanderers on the outside, lookers-in through windows at the magnified allurements of belonging and being welcome. 'A Disbelief', one of the best poems in The Pamphlet', is about this sudden, despairing sense of exile:

Love is a form of prayer; lost lost
a disbelief. No words from the faithless dark

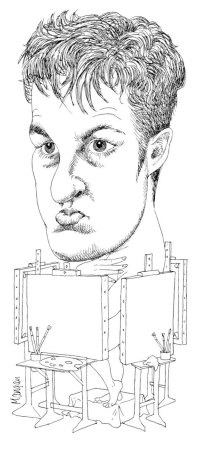

can mean. I had the key once,
opening the front door, calling your name.

The simplicity of the language works beautifully, because it is married to emotional truth. This is so with the following poem, 'Holloway Road', where love is lost through death rather than through estrangement. Duffy captures the power and the powerlessness of memory, which can bring the dead before us but cannot make them respond to us. The way she uses the tunnels of the Underground to echo the tunnels of the Underworld may not be new, but it is very effective, and so is the open, flowing quality of the short lines:

and remember as well
how you'd open the
                    door
with your head to one
                    side,
as though a joke
were half-way told
and the sight of a friend
was the punchline itself.

Duffy has included a couple of her 'World's Wife' poems in this pamphlet. Mrs Faust and Mrs Icarus take a suitably jaded view of their husbands. Probably these poems work better in performance than they do on the page, where they seem over-obvious, and a little laboured. Maurice Baring reinvented the classical drama rather similarly in his Diminutive Dramas, but the joke can wear thin, and in Duffy's case it doesn't seem the best use for her talent. The talent is so apparent, even in a patchy collection, that any falling-off is the more disappointing. However, this is an interim pamphlet, and very likely the next full collection will confirm the high place Duffy holds in the public mind and in private imaginations.

Tightwork

by Edwin Morgan

RICHARD PRICES
Perfume & Petrol Fumes
Diehard, £4.90
ISBN 0 946250 625

RICHARD PRICE, BORN in Reading but brought up in Scotland, and now working at the British Library in London, may perhaps be regarded as an Anglo-Scottish or Scoto-English poet, but labels do not suit him, and his poetry does not fit readily into currently discussed categories. It may be because of this that recognition was slower than it might have been, but his quality was noted by Carol Ann Duffy when she included him in her *Anvil New Poets 2* in 1995, and the present substantial collection, coming after several small pamphlets, will signal a very remarkable talent to readers who have not come across his work before.

In an essay printed in *Verse* in 1998, Price spoke of the importance of "very specific uses of language", and looked for a poetry that was "unafraid of speaking complicatedly, in tones of infinitesimal nuance". His own poetry is strong on nuance, and because the poems are mostly short they invite close attention. One or two of them are compressed almost to riddling status, but this is established as such a mark of intent that the reader is teased into the rewards of rereading. A recurrent theme is relationships of family and sex, where, as in life, what is not said, or half said, is as important as what is actually said, and the gaps, the repetitions, the phrases skating off into silence, the catspaw punctuation are deployed with great skill to keep a reader's mind active in tracing the tingly cataclysmic moves of love and anxiety.

> ... and the snow
> is just heavier than leaves,
> just more liquid,
> plural as millions et cetera –
> it's as fluid I mean
> as creamy falling stars
>
> and what falls between us

> falls and finishes the.
> "Bye," I say, say,
> and all of us, well, wave.
>
> ('As, as')

Social observation focuses sharply on beggars on Hungerford Bridge, a girl at a cashpoint seen from a bus, a driver adjusting the fuzzy sounds of his car radio without taking his eyes off the road. Sometimes, as in 'Horseshoe crab in flagrante delicto', imaginative observation lets an animal give a new (or very old) perspective on human behaviour. The female horseshoe crab (which is not a crab at all, but a "living fossil" related to spiders) slips out of the moonlit sea to do her million-year-old thing, and the poem cleverly uses the spider connection to make the sea a web which has already caught the struggling moon, waiting for the returning horseshoe crab to make for that anciently beckoning prey, having left her new life on the shores

> An abstract spider,
> she'll re-enter the fusses of the foam,
> see the glint in the deep
>
> and head for that struggling moon,
> the moon in the ocean's web,
> the moon's mime and its warning.

If the "petrol fumes" of the book's title can be sensed in some of the urban poems, the "perfume" makes an unexpected appearance in the prose poem 'Tights', where a precise eye unrolls the qualities and virtues of those clothes from packet to thigh, and becomes at the end a nose: "They are the closest clothes can be to being nothing without being nothing. They are the nearest fabric to perfume".

Of the longer poems, 'Lick and stick' is the most interesting, like a free extension of 'Tights', starting off from the second-skin patches of temporary tattoos, moving through clingfilm and gloves and lipgloss and pheromones and shampoo and underwear and woman-as-river imagery, and exfoliating into a sort of sensual celebration of all the layers of the flesh, "something to do with as close as possible / and still not knowing up to the minute". A considerable impetus is worked up, maybe at the expense of clarity but not unexciting.

An excellent book is rounded off by 'A Spelthorne Bird List', a series of short prose poems which fix the local bird life with a very beady eye.

REVIEWS

The Seventh Snooze

by Dennis O'Driscoll

TOMAS TRANSTRÖMER

New Collected Poems

Translated by Robin Fulton
Bloodaxe, £9.95
ISBN 1 85224 413 5

TOMAS TRANSTRÖMER, WHO was born in Stockholm in 1931, is a borderline poet. A typical poem by him will occur at the borders of sleep and waking, the conscious and the unconscious, the visible world and the otherworld. The Estonian poet, Jaan Kaplinski (whose book-titles, *The Wandering Border* and *Through the Forest*, encompass some of Tranströmer's own preoccupations), has written of the Swedish poet's ability "to reconcile and unite in his poetry many things that are considered opposites in our thinking" – modernism and traditionalism, internationalism and rootedness, realism and surrealism. Seamus Heaney (whose *Seeing Things* and *North* would be further contenders in any Tranströmer title contest) has found in Tranströmer – or "Trance-roamer" as he has been aptly called – a poet who cannot easily be pinned down, who is "equidistant from surrealist kitsch and post-modernist knowingness".

While difficulties in labelling Tranströmer suggest that he is agreeably unclassifiable, they also point to the vagueness and blandness which are characteristic of his less impressive poems. Of the many borders inhabited by his work, the frontier at which calmness of tone edges into inertness of style is the one where readers are most likely to involuntarily join their author in one of his near-sleep experiences. But Tranströmer is capable of more eye-opening poems on sleep, dreams, reveries and nightmares. The excellent 'Dream Seminar' compares the "annihilation" of the dream world by the act of waking to "when suspicious men / in uniforms stop the tourist – / open his camera, unwind the film / and let the daylight kill the pictures". Another memorable image for coming to consciousness appears in the opening lines of 'Deep in Europe':

I a dark hull between two lock-gates
rest in the hotel bed while the city around me
　　　　　　　　　　　　　　　　　　wakens.
The silent clamour and the grey light stream in
and raise me slowly to the next level: the morning.

Tranströmer's imagistic ingenuity is one of his strengths, adding depth to some poems, lifting others to new and unexpected dimensions. "Like", "as if", "as when" – images cluster around his poems like moths "on the window pane: / small pale telegrams from the world". New York is "a spiral galaxy seen from the side"; unanswered letters "pile up, like cirro-stratus clouds promising bad weather"; an excavator parked with its "scoop against the earth" resembles "a man who has fallen asleep at table / with his fist in front of him". Also a poet of surprising conjunctions, Tranströmer draws together a rusting tug and a sprouting mushroom, "sooty palm-trees / and the train whistle's flurrying / silver-white bats"; some of his most convincing poems are layered with contrasting images like successive coats of paint, each a shade different from the next, each layer altering in mood or colour those which have gone before. His most familiar poem, 'Tracks', uses this multi-layered technique in describing a train stopped at 2 a.m. "out in the middle of the plain". Notwithstanding its static subject, the poem travels a long way in eleven lines, capturing the bleak 2 a.m. atmosphere and the comfortless associations of that forlorn hour ('As when someone has gone into an illness so deep / everything his days were becomes a few flickering points, a swarm, / cold and tiny at the horizon'). The stalled train provides a vehicle – as do cars in other Tranströmer poems – for a meditation on existential isolation and that state of habitual human "betweenness" of which he is a tireless chronicler.

If 'Tracks' is his best-known poem, 'Baltics' – published sixteen years later, in 1974 – is Tranströmer's best, a "truth...lifted out of silence". Nothing written by him before or since 'Baltics' combines such sustained energy, such tonal range, such narrative interest. The six-part poem sets out to preserve the evanescent, to record the lives of the near-forgotten, to find a way of "writing a long letter to the dead" (not least to his grandparents, whose intuitive traits are implicitly linked with his own artistic gifts). Tranströmer's five brief collections since 'Baltics' (at full stretch, he makes up in intensity what he lacks in quantity) resume his evocation of vatic and visionary moments, unexpected epiphanies, insights which come as close to religious revelations as a secular age and a reticent temperament will permit:

> I am an anchor that has dug itself down and holds
>   steady
> the huge shadow floating up there,
> the great unknown which I am a part of and which is
>   certainly more
> important than me.

This welcome update of an earlier *Collected Poems* (1987), also translated by Robin Fulton, ends with a series of episodic childhood reminiscences in prose which are as piquant as the ethyl acetate odour which pervaded Tranströmer's insect-collecting youth. Much the most important short chapter is the one called 'Exorcism', revealing that "During the winter when I was fifteen I was afflicted by a severe form of anxiety... The world was a vast hospital. I saw before me human beings deformed in body and in soul". Typically, Tranströmer tells his story in an unfussy, unsensational style; but, even without his admission that the sustained anguish inflicted by this haunting was "possibly my most important experience", one would guess, both from the content of a number of poems and from his choice of profession (he worked as a psychologist until 1990), how formative this visitation has been. Painful faultlines are everywhere discernible between the lines of Tranströmer's lonely and quietly disturbing work:

> I close my eyes.
> There is a soundless world
> there is a crack
> where dead people
> are smuggled across the border.

Myth Mixer

by Ruth Padel

LINDA PASTAN
Carnival Evening
New and Selected Poems 1968-1998
Norton, USA $27.50

LINDA PASTAN'S SPECIALITY is putting a mythological filter on domestic life. The earliest poem in this book, describing a journey home for Christmas ("and a house / wrapped as safely in scenery / as the corn in its layers of husk") is called 'Arcadia'. Thirty years on, she is comparing domestic happiness and its difficulties to "rites", or to gold coins alchemized by Midas. In 'The Obligation to be Happy', one of the most recent poems, the titular obligation "is more onerous/than the rites of beauty / or housework, harder than love", yet the poet lives with someone who expects it of her "casually, / the way you expect the sun to come up". Wearing happiness like a rucksack "heavy with gold coins", she stumbles "around the house, / I bump into things. / Only Midas himself / would understand".

So all through this *New and Selected*, nine collections worth plus the last three years' work, Pastan beams the Bible, Greek myth and ritual onto relationships – between spouses, fathers and daughters, mothers and daughters – and onto activities like weaving, laundry and childcare. Politics too. In 'Libation, 1966', boys going off to the Vietnam jungle are compared to sacrificial scapegoats of ancient ritual:

> We used to sacrifice young girls
> killing them like does
> on rocky altars
> they themselves had kept
> tidy as kitchens...
>
> Now we give young men.
> They dance as delicately
> as any bull boy, with bayonet
> in a green maze,
> under a sky hot as Crete.

More subtly, perhaps, and less explanatorily, animals carry their own myths under the skin of a poem:

> the children holding the python
> all along its ten-foot mottled body
> are like the blind men with the elephant -
> what can they know
> of what they hold beneath their fingers...?

There is a strong urge round here to explain; and you might notice this is territory without much irony or self-humour. "We have chosen the dangerous life" runs one line in 'Who Is It Accuses Us?' from a 1981 collection: a poem which claims that housewives live most dangerously of all. "You who risk no more than your own skins / I tell you household gods / are jealous gods". Her 'Circe' announces "My men will moan and dream of me / for years". The domestic myth has a slightly tub-thumping echo.

Her work does have delicate conceits and soft-tissue images of female life: "threads to be woven later" is an archetypal busy-mum-desperate-to-turn-to-lyric-in-a-moment-of-longed-for-solitude poem – in low-case, to signal the unnoticed, undervalued demandingness of the housebound life in which you have no time for external conventions like capital letters. "the baby's head / fragile as a moon... / in my son's writing / the mother is the villain / the year / I took to my typewriter / as others take to their bed".

But there is not much self-critical play here in the matter of rhythm and cadence, either; and this dearth of worked-at music, or any clear sound-shape, somehow affects the poems' conceptual movement. Take the lines "Perhaps God / listed what to create / in a week" (from 'Lists', in a 1982 collection). What can you do with a single line like "listed what to create"? It has no forward movement, is as bathetic as the "perhaps" that opens the not-very-interesting thought; and the jerky, quick-muted lines, combined with those hissy Ts and the loose indirect question, all give the impression of a pilot who doesn't much care what she's doing, soundwise or conceptwise, at the helm.

But I don't want to be unfair, and it is too easy to criticize from the other side of the Atlantic. Linda Pasten was Poet Laureate of Maryland from 1991-1993; she is best at describing concrete human landscapes without over-egging the myth or weighing things down with philosophical questioning. 'Dreaming of Rural America', a recent poem, stretches a deep hurt sympathy over the land she knows intimately – its physical history, its wind and smell and textures, and the interior tragedies of its inhabitants:

> I want to enter the ticking heart
> of the country and in a rented car
> drive for miles past fields scored
> with the history of wind; past
> silos, those inland lighthouses,
> where corn smolders to golden dust.
> I want an RD number and a tin mailbox
> filled with flowers instead of letters...
> In the dream
> of rural America, farmers have lost
> the knack of despair. They do not
> breathe the diesel fumes of whiskey
> into the faces of their women.
> They do not wield their leather belts
> to erase, on the backs of their sons,
> the old stigmata of failure.

Print Cull

by Adam Thorpe

D.J. ENRIGHT
Play Resumed
Oxford, £18
ISBN 0 19 288108 6

COMMONPLACE BOOKS ARE out of fashion, at least in Britain; perhaps our newspapers and their heft of supplements have made them redundant. Two of my favourite twentieth-century writers are Pessoa and Cioran, masters of casual aphorism, but their continental seriousness (like Ralph Waldo Emerson's) has no real counterpart over here; the essence of the commonplace book is its embracing of the trite as well as the notable. Anything goes, anything goes in, and at the end we might just have a feel for the person behind it.

D.J. Enright calls his a "journal", but a journal is a record of days, and only occasionally here do we glimpse a life rather than an opinion (though I can already hear him wondering what I mean by "life"). Enright isn't overtly opinionated. Reflection rarely hardens into aphorism (if it's aphorism you want) and impatience with, say, the dafter elements of political correctness never boils into passion. Even his hospital experience is more amusing than sad, though there is one astonishing exception:

> The valley of the shadow of death, through which
> the NHS conducts us with wandering steps and
> slow, seems interminable. We are sorry, we are too
> many.

That has a Larkinian ring to it, the knell of ghastly truth – the Biblical epic set beside the messy squalor of the everyday. Despite Enright's fondness for Nietzsche, Schopenhauer or Kierkegaard, the journal remains resolutely "ordinary" and modest. The good poet, he puts a twist on what we have already thought: if Sunday's former dullness prepared us well for work, its present open-at-all-hours excitement, "celebrated by newspapers starring varieties of sexual experience... spoils one for... Monday". He is fond of misprints and misprisions and exam howlers, collecting them like quirky butterflies. When he delightedly reads "Life isn't a television aerial" for "Life isn't a television serial" and reflects that he was "reading rather better than the author wrote", he comes close to sounding like Stanley Fish. But he is allergic to most forms of trendy theory, as he is to needless technological advance. Bemoaning the proliferation of letters and numbers on letterheads, he gives us a wonderful quote from Karl Kraus: "Technology is a servant who makes so much noise cleaning up in the next room that his master cannot make music". Slightly frustrating, then, that he fails to muse further on the source of this derangement. I wanted a bit of old-fashioned ire, a sprinkle of Lear amongst the jottings, even the kind of dotty extremism that makes Alan Clark's diaries so riveting. Even when he appears to be suggesting capital punishment as the answer for child murderers and abusers, Enright blames this disproportion on old age.

Much of his trawl is, in fact, taken from the newspapers, especially *The Times* letters page. Even a "rubbishy" supplement yields an *aperçu* from Georges Simenon on writing's "vocation of unhappiness" – nevertheless, Simenon "published over 400 books". Neither is he afraid of a section devoted to *Eastenders* and *Coronation Street*, making the poignant suggestion that, deprived of community life and all its "wrangling" and "spying", we crouch to an artifical one. The typical Enright twist is to conclude that "we are very glad we have no share in it". What might have been a contemporary regret becomes, well, the last line of an unformed poem, with a good poem's scuttling away from the received idea. Indeed, many of these paragraphs might well have taken their station among the prose poems found in his collections.

Cioran and Emerson pop up several times, as well as Goethe, Borges and Henri-Frédéric Amiel, whose *Journal intime* is quoted from as an epigraph – perhaps unwisely, since Amiel's masterpiece was an escape from despair and futility. Cioran is criticised for writing too much, but praised for his ambiguity of tone – "you can't always tell whether he is extolling or excoriating". Excoriation is more exciting to read, of course, than Enright's mild English put-down. He is best when poker-faced – picking out, for instance, the consumerist nastiness of the Blairite statement, "'If we abuse children we abuse our own future' (It might be thought sufficient to say, If we abuse children, we abuse children)". His main quarry is this sort of thing, finding much material for comment in the kind of brochures that fall to your feet out of the daily paper. He is interesting on translation, too, having revised Kilmartin's revision of Scott-Moncrieff's translation of Proust: a Borgesian deed, as is having to review a commonplace book punctuated with sharp comments on reviewers.

Written in his Blood

by Atar Hadari

MICHAEL ONDAATJE
Handwriting
Bloomsbury, £9.99
ISBN 0 7475 4261 9

THE CENTRAL IMAGE in these three sequences of poems is one of burial, unearthment and renewal – of statues of the Buddha, of water, of emotions, memories, a life that counts. Ondaatje starts us on this road of memories from his childhood home of Sri Lanka with a series of historical anecdotes and details, a place where "We believed in the intimate life, an inner self" and "3am in temples, the hour of washing the gods" led to a God being dragged from temples "by one's own priests" to be buried while wars, treasure hunters and fifty-year feuds went by, so that "roots / like the fingers of a blind monk / spread for two hundred years over his face".

In the third and most anecdotally direct, least oblique sequence, the image of the dug up Buddha reappears transformed: "In the sunless forest /of Ritagala.. .nine soldiers on leave / strip uniforms off / and dig a well... / In the sunless forest / crouched by a forest well / pulling what was lost out of the depth". And immediately before that anecdote, in one of the achingly simple lyrics that litter this thatched basket of stories and semi-parables, Ondaatje tells of "the last Sinhala word" he lost, "the word for water" and the wet nurse "a lost almost-mother in those years /of thirsty love" who he has no photograph of, has not seen since age eleven, whose grave he hears none tell. He now wonders who abandoned whom.

Now and then the concerns of a writer surface and you realise these are the meditations of one returning to buried wounds and springs to be renewed: the poets who "slept, famous, in palace courtyards /then hid within forests when they were hunted /...and were killed and made wore famous". Or in the second sequence "The Nine Sentiments", which corresponds to the nine sentiments of Indian love poetry (romantic/erotic, humorous, pathetic, angry, heroic, fearful, disgustful, amazed and peaceful – as I'm sure you wanted to know) there comes this very modern unease: "Where is the forest / not cut down / for profit or literature.." and lines later "Where is there a room / without the damn god of love?"

These poems are of the haunted and of the haunting, of what you cannot escape from, and when Ondaatje uses techniques of Indian poetry, even language and references you do not as a Westerner recognise such is the sensual certainty of his grasp that you take them on faith. He will talk of what you do not know and then of "gold ragas of longing / like lit sequin / on her shifting green dress". I will fall under Ondaatje's daze as he recalls what was lost in his own half dreaming sleep.

Where the poems take longest to work their magic is in the opening, where you do not have a framework of emotions to connect all these anecdotes to and the details may seem merely colourful. As the book progresses he unpacks before you both the good and the bad memories, the pains of history and personal loss and the quick, effortless watercolours capturing exotic scenes like some British traveller of the last century or before – of "women of the Boralesgamuwa" singing "songs to celebrate the washing of arms and bangles...the three folds on their stomachs / considered a sign of beauty" on afternoons when husbands are away and they "try out all their ankle bracelets". And in some pure love lyrics his style becomes that of the imitated so there is no more than a hair's breadth between him and the model, not a crack to see light through between him and the heights of, say, Arthur Waley's classic Chinese poetry translations in lines like: "her fearless heart / light as a barn owl / against him all night". In the closing poem 'Last Ink' Ondaatje closes in on what remains: "the dusk light, the cloud pattern, / recorded always in your heart / and the rest of the world – chaos, / circling your winter boat".

A central poem of the first section starts simply with the line: "What we lost". This he continues to catalogue in some detail as a whole way of life, of civilisation and love and ways of loving "burned or traded for power and wealth". The rest, he concludes, is only love. And momentary, sought out opportunities for leaps and bowing.

Acting Sincerity

by Michael Hulse

MICHAEL HOFMANN
Approximately Nowhere
Faber, £7.99
ISBN 0 571 19524 5

IN *ACRIMONY* (1986) Michael Hofmann observed the "beaverish wrinkles of feeding or disdain" around his father's nose and mouth, registered Gert Hofmann's "salami breath" and "overloud, forced bonhomie" and his "interviewee's too-rapid turning to his own experience", and wondered "what sort of consummation is available? / Fight; talk literature and politics; get drunk together? // Kiss him goodnight, as though half my life had never happened?" The son and his celebrated novelist father and the Anglo-German cross-over made good copy, and TV, which loves the dynastic, duly made the documentary.

Then on 1 July 1993 Gert Hofmann died; and in a poem that appeared in *The Observer* and in a limited edition (no, not by Squirrelprick Press) in Holland and was subsequently broadcast with the rest of the group of valedictory poems on Radio 3, the son is seen in that moment we all face, confronted with the emptiness where the dead father ought to be but no longer is:

> The window atilt, the blinds at
>   half-mast,
> the straw star swinging in the
>   draught, and my father
> for once not at his post, not in the
>   penumbra
> frowning up from his
>   manuscript at the world.

For the father with whom relations in life were complex, the son feels grief: on this bedrock of experience, mercifully, the poems in the opening part of this new book rest, expressing at times the tenderness that the earlier book kept at bay. Death, after all, is the great change. Still, some things are not changed, not least because it is not honest that they should be. One is Michael Hofmann's caustic choice of detail: "The same books as for years, the only additions by himself", he notes in his father's study (in that same opening poem). Another is the tendency, partly inherited from his poetic father, Robert Lowell, to make Literature (nothing as plain as just poems of grief) out of his personal loss. The most problematic poem in the first part of *Approximately Nowhere* must surely be 'Epithanaton', which goes to the heart of farewell from the dead – the father visited in his open coffin, the cremation – and is moving when it is at its simplest ("I hardly dared touch you"). But this poem of all poems is filled with mere Literature – from its title, through its reflections on famous last words, through the thought that "the Russian (Tolstoy or Dostoevsky, ask Steiner)" wrote something about the sharper features of the dead, through creative writing phrase-making ("pluperfect flowers"), to its concluding six lines, where the allusions and wordplay drag truthful feeling into the mire of cleverness:

> Like a cavalier swain, I speared my flowers at my feet,
> a no-throw, the *blaue Blume* of the Romantics,
>   delphiniums,
>
> blue for faith, and turned on my heel,
> prematurely, unconscionably, leaving you behind.
> Then, while my back was turned, you went up in
>   smoke, more *dicke Luft*.

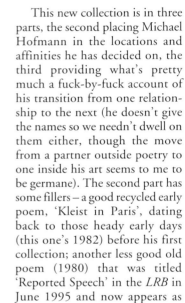

This new collection is in three parts, the second placing Michael Hofmann in the locations and affinities he has decided on, the third providing what's pretty much a fuck-by-fuck account of his transition from one relationship to the next (he doesn't give the names so we needn't dwell on them either, though the move from a partner outside poetry to one inside his art seems to me to be germane). The second part has some fillers – a good recycled early poem, 'Kleist in Paris', dating back to those heady early days (this one's 1982) before his first collection; another less good old poem (1980) that was titled 'Reported Speech' in the *LRB* in June 1995 and now appears as 'Vecchi Versi' (a poem on his father has changed too, from 'Doctors' to 'Beatitudes' – one day the academics will have fun with the dates, titles and other compositional minutiae of Hofmann's poems); and some too-slight quasi-Roman marginalia ('Essex', 'Ingerlund', 'Parerga'). One poem is written in memoriam Joseph Brodsky and another, dedicated to James Lasdun, features a snapshot of Brodsky in a Tottenham Court Road Café, "sitting in the window / with paper and a cigarette, / the recording angel, / miles away". Another poem, 'Hotel New York, Rotterdam', is dedicated to a hotel fetishist, the German poet Joachim Sartorius, now the Goethe Institute supremo and also the man who put Hofmann and Lavinia Greenlaw into his hugely influential anthology of contemporary world poetry, making them the only two younger British poets known to German readers. Two poems describe the university patch at Gainesville, Florida, where Hofmann teaches creative writing.

All very lit-biz.

From all of these poems, as from those in the more interesting first and third parts of the book, an overriding position emerges: this (reader) is how the facts of my life are, and it is adult of me to take them whole, down to the "stubs in the lid of a jam-jar" or "a syringe for afters" or "I piss in bottles". An understanding that human maturity must mean truthfulness has always been seminal to Michael Hofmann's poetry (thank God). He is in fact one of the few poets around who write for grown-ups. He doesn't pander to the types who teach post-this-or-that courses or to tastes for grotesquerie or so-called magic: for this relief much thanks. And still, the admiration I've always had for his work is tempered, on reading this book, by finding the character "Michael Hofmann" too knowingly played, all "his" very male and existential and fractious literary coordinates (Camus, Brodsky, the Hemingway of *A Moveable Feast*) too assertively in place, the truthfulness too much paraded. To uphold an unqualified admiration I could fall back on Trilling's contention, in *Sincerity and Authenticity*, that the sincere man, in order to be understood in his sincerity, may find himself having to *act* sincerity. And I'm trying to read *Approximately Nowhere* in that spirit, heaven knows I'm trying.

The poems of sexual obsession in the third part of the book challenge the attempt. Unquestionably they are well-written. They are frank and taut and fully recognisable ("I keep my balls / coddled in your second-best lace panties"); they show sexual wanting so it feels like desire and not just words, and that is a lot; they say, "I was living on air, cigarettes, pull-ups and kisses" and I believe it. Hofmann is so much more readable on this subject than any other poet who's recently tried it that it feels perverse to be dissatisfied, but I am, and I think it's because these poems come at me with too great an awareness of making Literature on the wing, out of the rawness of what happens as it happens. And it's also for what may be a poor reason, a sentimental more than a moral reflex: I find myself thinking of the woman left aside in that summer of looking for shady patches of grass and pulling on the phone like a bottle and fetching up "jubilant, a seesaw at rest, not one foot on the floor", the woman who perhaps read the poems promptly published in the *LRB* as the rest of us did and who may have her own ideas on the last line of 'Is it decided' (*LRB* 21 July 1994): "I'm in mourning for my life – or ours; or ours?" Is this legitimate comment in a reviewer? Where (pardon this wretched question) should Literature end and Life be left its due? Michael Hofmann, presumably with the consent of those concerned, has given his answer. I think his answer is the right one; but part of me hates myself, and him, for thinking that way.

CHARLES TOMLINSON
BREAD AND STONE

The fragment of a loaf, rejected, stale:
As beautiful as any stone, it bears
Seams, scars, a dust of flour and like a stone,
If it could unfold its history,
Would speak of its time in darkness and of light
Drawing it towards the thing it is,
Hard to the hand, an obstacle to sight,
Out of an untold matrix. If a son
Ask bread of you, would stone be your reply?
Let the differentiating eye
Rest on this, and for the moment read
The seed of nourishment in it as the sun
Reveals this broken bread as textured stone,
Served out as a double feast for us
On the cloth of the commonplace miraculous.

ANDREW WATERMAN
PLAY THAT THING

Soon I'd no need to play it, though I'd often
Put on, it anyway would happen
Inside my head, and everywhere I'd listen.

It seemed the city's pulse, the groan and strum
Of escalators, and tunnels as trains came
Pushing its fizz down the live rail before them.

I walked out to the bypass, windscreens flashed
Staccato riffs of sun as cars streamed past,
And every way for miles still rooflines, vast

Chains of tarmac, brick and concrete bound
The suffocated hills; the music mourned
And sizzled, syncopated and profound.

A last road studded with rich mansions lifted
Me to the top, some stars; but when I looked at
The valley beyond, more drifts of suburb choked it.

Then round night's ridge, first kindled threads and slivers,
Then merged to flame, in which trumpet's bravura
Scarlets, indigo trombone slidings, silver

Clarinet filigree blazed to what black dots
Swarming staves could never replicate:
Like lava it crescendoed, and as hot.

And what I saw was not old Storyville's
Distant demolished brothels, drinking-halls,
Nor Mississippi-churning paddle-wheels,

Just black faces bent to instruments, the offspring
Of slaves, if now called free yet still possessing
Nothing, pouring forth heart's hurts and blessings

Under a huge full moon, the blue expansion
Of plain around lit by bright constellations
That met it with no visible horizon.

ELIZABETH BARTLETT
PUSHKIN

No, don't make a mistake, he did not write.
He was just a writer's cat, who came
on an angel-visit, that delightful intercourse
of short duration. His literary name,
his stilted walk, his slight fawn body,
and his blue eyes staring from that strange
dark mask, those affected brown suede boots,
had the other cats, who didn't like change
of any kind, falling about laughing.

In their defence it has be said
that many turned up in black fur
when word got round that he was dead.
Others wandered by in gold or grey,
with cobby peasant heads and legs,
padding across the mounded turf,
and urinated daily where he lay.

MICHAEL HENRY
CAMBRIAN RAIN

Where are those rains? The Celtic rains
that used to drift in from the sea?
And the people who drowned in holes of rain?

A South American combo
is playing *Guantanamera*,
mandolin-strings across Cardiff Bay.

Houses have put their evening glasses on.
A spectral corporation-cream bus
drives past: direction nowhere.

Stores loom out of a *film noir* glaze,
their disconnected displays
pageants of the absurd.

Tesco's turns on hedgerows of spangled light.
I can smell the honeyed buddleia of lost summers,
drizzling through the half-rose of Orion's Belt

and what seemed faraway seems close.
My wipers can do nothing with the rain,
running bloodshot through a hole of tears.

HUGH MACPHERSON
NIGHT WALKING

Late night walking, midnight walking:
I pause to take my bearings, step through
dark that's intimate and emphatic,
more real than the blocks of light that hang
from lamp-posts in strange geometric
declarations of space: hard to believe
one can walk through those unscathed.

While the dark itself is soft and accommodating,
breathing gently in my ear with slow rhythm
of pines, or grasses blown by river breeze.
I don't stop as I leave the village, dazzled by
windows with lamps and flowers, pleased
by scenes where the family's glimpsed around the table,
odd lighted corners of rooms I've come to know,

better than the owners themselves, as each evening
shows me the same unconsidered angles of calm
and shade. How many stories and dreams surge up
at these visions – memories, fantasies, virtual friendships
that tact forgets as next day fails to merge with
the night world. But now in any case
all the woods shift subtly around me

as I reach the pines and the dark
mingles on familiar terms with trees,
introducing me to scents and textures
of barks and cones that it's long moved among,
pressing them to my hands now as I falter
before these new, demanding friends.
Silence now among the trees and moss

– but one that's contemplative, companionable:
where nothing is said because you feel at ease.
The dark, having made the introduction,
withdraws a little way while the night
becomes luminous as my eyes refine their vision.
All around the world spins its burden of lives, while
the darkness approves, and whispers confirmation.

PETE MORGAN
GOOD ORTS

The working worm, the wind, the rain
unearth the reawakening
in broken blinks of porcelain –
the delft, the crackleware, the spode;
in gobs of glass, in shives of bone –
the rat, the chicken, and the ox.

To shift the earth with iron assists
the wrench of root, the slow upheave
which turns today from yesterday –
the crack of crockery, the clink
of metal against metal's blight –
"GEORGIVS V DEI GRA:BRITT:"

Reverse; Brittania, verdigris –
the shield worn thin by years of spin
against the grindings of a ground
which rises in a rising tide
of snicks and snippets, sharp shiveens
of some lost sorrow swallowing

the light of rediscovery.
The pieces never fit, no chip
of china fits the next dull crock
of earthenware returned to earth.
No metal lets the secret free
but *they* return, reflected in

the ownership of shattered finds –
the cup, the candlestick, the urn,
the lock, the key, the broken bell
which clangs one off-key on the earth
uttered with smithers of good orts
wink their thousand eyes at rain.

NEWS/COMMENT

GEOFFREY DEARMER PRIZE

This year's Geoffrey Dearmer Prize, for poets published in *Poetry Review* who have yet to publish a book, will be judged by Sheenagh Pugh. The shortlisted poets are: Ros Barber, R. G. Binns, V. G. Lee, Angela Leighton, Hugh Macpherson, Cate Parish and Sarah Wardle. Work from the shortlisted poets will be featured in the next issue and the winner will be announced on National Poetry Day, October 7th.

POBOOKS ON LINE

Given the poor availability of poetry in bookshops in many parts of the country, the coming of Internet bookselling ought to be a real boost for poetry. The stocks held by sites such as Amazon and BOL, the two biggest sites are enormous. When rare titles are listed but not in stock, they will obtain them within 4-6 weeks but it's usually quicker. To allow for postage most titles are discounted. One of Amazon's most useful features is its sales ratings, given automatically when a search throws up a title, and its bestseller lists. In its early days the Amazon joke was that any author could order a copy of his or her own book and watch its ratings soar by thousands of places. These days the volume is somewhat higher. Interestingly, 34 titles in the poetry top 50 are exclusively 20th-century poetry, denting somewhat an old chestnut about the unsaleability of work after 1900.

NET VERSE

Things change rapidly on the web, so I'll mention some sites that show promise, but are still under construction as I write.

The new Welsh Academi web site at http://www.academi.org looks as if it could become a immensely valuable noticeboard for poetry in Wales. It already has events listings and information about the Ty Newydd writing centre, and placeholders for stuff on residencies, publications and more.

David Kennedy has started a personal site at http://www.geocities.com/SoHo/Atrium/6516. This has some uncollected poetry, criticism and a fascinating experimental page of Cut-ups, Foldins, and BatMemes.

Sound Eye at http://indigo.ie/~tjac/sound_eye_index.htm declares itself to be concerned with Irish Poetry & the Universe of Writing. It has an events list (which needed updating when I visited) and samples of poetry from Maurice Scully, Brian Coffey, Trevor Joyce and others. It's interesting, but needs a bit more work to live up to its aspirations.

Poetry newsgroups ought to be a good idea, but don't seem to work in practice. More successful are the poetry mailing lists that have been springing up recently. Perhaps it's because they have a nominal owner, who can influence the tone and direction of each list. An unusual one is Mairead Byrne's *Ictus*. On many lists, discussion of war and poetry is controversial, but this one was set up just for that purpose. If that interests you, visit http://ictus.listbot.com to join.

Flash fiction is a condensed form of writing somewhere between prose poetry and short stories, and it seems to be growing in popularity on the Web. If you want to investigate it, the *Furious Fictions* site at http://www.slip.net/%7Effiction/index.html is a good place to start. And if you like your stories really short, try *Story Bytes* at http://thor.he.net/~stories/ where all the stories have word lengths of a power of two.

Send brief tales of other interesting sites to peter@hphoward.demon.co.uk

CORREX

Australian poet Pam Brown's website, listed in the last issue, has moved to http://www.geocities.com/Soho/Workshop/7629

FORTHCOMING ISSUES

Autumn

An Encounter with Ted Hughes by Carolyne Wright

Geoffrey Dearmer shortlisted poets featured

Poems by James Lasdun, Billy Collins, Matthew Francis, Connie Bensley, Rita Ann Higgins, Peter Redgrove, Fred Voss

Reviews of Michael Schmidt's *Harvill Book of Twentieth-Century Poetry in English, Russian Poetry in a New Era,* **Don Paterson, Sophie Hannah, Ciaran Carson, Adam Thorpe.**

LETTERS

CATHOLIC EDUCATION

Dear Peter,

I suppose I should buy Peter Porter an orange sash for his doughty fight against my terrible Catholicism, in your Australian issue (Vol 89/1, p.11). In fact my politics are almost entirely concerned with something else. I worry and speak about relegated persons and groups, from those whom fashion is deployed against to victims of genocide. This was what made the end of my *New Oxford Book of Australian Verse* different from Porter's *Oxford Anthology*. As well as some of the Gramscian and post-Gramscian poets it and your *Review* rightly honour, my Oxbook, as I call it, also included work from poets whom our Gramscian orthodoxy proscribes. May I also defend John Whitworth? He's in fact a much better poet than his piece in *PR* 89/1 would suggest.

Yours sincerely,
LES MURRAY
Bunyah, New South Wales

THE SOCIETY OF AUTHORS

Eric Gregory Awards 2000

Annual awards totalling up to £24,000 for the encouragement of young poets.

A candidate must be British by birth, under the age of 30, and may submit a published or unpublished volume of poetry
(up to 30 poems).

Closing date 31 October 1999.

Full details and entry form from:
Awards Secretary, The Society of Authors,
84 Drayton Gardens, London SW10 9SB.
Please send SAE.

SOME CONTRIBUTORS

Peter Bland's *Selected Poems* were published by Carcanet last year.
Charles Boyle's latest collection is *Paleface* (Faber).
Stephen Burt's work appears in Carcanet's *New Poetries 2*, just out.
Kate Clanchy's new collection, *Samarkand*, is forthcoming from Picador.
Claudio Damiani was born in 1957. He has published two collections.
Eugene Dubnov was born in Estonia in 1949 and has lived in England since 1975.
Helen Dunmore's latest novel is *Your Blue-Eyed Boy* (Penguin).
Roberto Galaverni is the editor of *Nuovi Poeti Italiani Contemporanei* (Guaraldi).
Alla Gelich was born in Moscow and came to England in 1975 after her detention by the KGB.
Andrea Gibellini was born in 1965. His first collection *Le ossa di Bering* was published in 1993.
Atar Hadari was a featured new poet in *PR* Vol 86 No 1, 1996.
Mark Halliday's books, *Tasker Street* and *Little Star* are available in the UK at Waterstone's, Manchester.
Zbigniew Herbert died last year; an appreciation appeared in Vol 88 No 4.
Michael Hulse is now editing *Stand* (with John Kinsella).
James Keery's first collection *That Stranger, The Blues* was published by Carcanet in 1997.
Valerio Magrelli was born in 1957. He has published three collections.
Edwin Morgan's *Collected Poems* are published by Carcanet.
Andrew Motion's latest collection is *Poems 1976–1997* (Faber).
Dennis O'Driscoll's forthcoming collection, *Weather Permitting* (Anvil), is a PBS Autumn Recommendation.
Ruth Padel's latest collection is *Rembrandt Would Have Loved You* (Chatto).
Justo Jorge Padrón's *On the Cutting Edge*, translated by Louis Bourne, was published by Forest in 1998.
Tom Paulin's new collection, *The Wind Dog*, is forthcoming from Faber.
M. R. Peacocke's latest collection is *Selves* (Peterloo, 1995).
Sheenagh Pugh's new collection is *Stonelight* (Seren). The entire Fanfic sequence can be found on her website x-stream.fortunecity.com/sonicst/68/
Davide Rondoni was born in 1964. He has published four collections.
Carol Rumens' collection of her Irish poems, *holding pattern*, was published by Blackstaff last year.
Frances Sackett's first collection, *The Hand Glass*, was published by Seren in 1996.
Linda Saunders is associate Editor of *Modern Painters*.
Robert Saxton's first collection *The Promise Clinic* is published by Enitharmon.
Vernon Scannell's latest collection is *The Black and White Days* (Robson Books).
Piotr Sommer's *Poems to Translate* is published by Bloodaxe.
Adam Thorpe's third collection, *From the Neanderthal*, is just out from Cape.
Georg Trakl (1887-1914) was an Austrian poet who committed suicide as a result of his experiences in the First World War. 'Grodek' was his last poems, written during the battle of the same name in Galicia. A collection of Margitt Lehbert's translations is forthcoming from Anvil.